Anxiety and Stress: an A-Z for Beginners

Dr. Jerry Kennard is a Chartered Psychologist and Associate Fellow of the British Psychological Society. He is an established health blogger and author of self-help books. He currently contributes regular blogs to Remedy Health Media and is the former Men's Health Guide to About.com..

Dr. Kennard began his career in mental health and worked in a variety of settings. Two decades on he moved into higher education where he subsequently headed a university department of psychology. He lives close to the City of York in the United Kingdom. Jerry can be contacted via his website: jerrykennard.net.

Additional Titles by Dr. Jerry Kennard

Bipolar Disorder: a short introductory guide
Bipolar Disorder: a student's guide
Overcoming Worry and Anxiety (Sheldon Press)
Panic Attacks: a short introductory guide to panic and its management

Anxiety and Stress

An A-Z for Beginners

Dr. Jerry Kennard. CPsychol., AFBPsS

"To grapple with and understand anxiety is, in some sense, to grapple with and understand the human condition."

Scott Stossel

CONTENTS

About this book

There are plenty of choices available when it comes to books on anxiety and stress. They tend to fall into either academic or self-help categories and I've nothing against either. This book is a little different. It isn't academic, but it is informed academically, and it isn't a self-help book in the true sense of the word. So what is it?

The title holds the clue. We all know of the existence of anxiety and stress but how many of us know just how influential they are on our lives, our work, our relationships with others and the things we do? I've provided an A-Z of anxiety and stress related issues. It doesn't cover everything (I'd need a few volumes for that) so much as it identifies examples of typical everyday issues most people can identify with.

To this end the book will be useful to anyone with a curiosity as to the general nature and effects of anxiety and stress. It provides brief insights into the complexities, the mechanisms and the sheer enormity of issues in our lives that are influenced and affected by anxiety and stress. Whether you start at the beginning and work your way through or just dip into the chapters that stir your curiosity, you should, I hope, find something of interest.

Jerry Kennard.

Introduction

This book is about anxiety and stress and I'm introducing it by the simple acknowledgment that we live in stressful times. I'm also identifying some of the things we can do to turn things around. As previously mentioned, this isn't really a self-help book although from time to time I do illustrate the process of change we might use in certain circumstances. Equally, I don't want to leave anyone with the impression that we are helpless victims of anxiety and stress. The key to coping is to identify those things in life we can do something about. So let's begin by seeing which of the following you can connect with:

Never being wrong. Sometimes this is a self-imposed issue rather than a reality but we do also live in times when mistakes, even relatively mild ones, are viewed with scorn. There's a tension here in that we accept modest levels of error, from a new employee for example, but after that the world of work can be an unforgiving place.

More-for-less. Every place I've ever worked goes through the remorseless business of reorganization. After all the upheaval I'm left with a feeling that two things have resulted. The first is that everyone has gone through huge and often unnecessary levels of stress. The second is that work roles become organized in such a way that what was once the job two people did, now becomes the task for one person. Needless to say the effects of such changes rarely, in my view, seem to achieve what the multi-page justification said it would.

Pushed and Pulled in Different Directions. Very often it's the conflicting demands made of us that causes stress. These days, for example, I work for myself. In one respect it's great but like all freelancers I often experience the conflict of knowing I could do with time off, but needing to work. I have a deadline to meet but I must also keep my promise to visit my sister today and I must remember to collect a parcel from the depot. Working for myself may sound great but there's very little slack for vacations or illness. Your situation may be different but our daily lives are filled with such issues and sometimes it forces us to make choices.

Giving and Taking. In order to operate successfully we really need to be surrounded by people who treat us in ways they would like to be treated. We'd like some support, some trust and some give-and-take. Unfortunately there are people who are only too prepared to take and others who, perhaps willingly or otherwise, are the givers. If by nature you are something of a giver you will almost certainly find people in your orbit who are only too willing to take. It almost certainly places too many physical and emotional demands on the giver.

Relationships. By this I'm thinking of intimate relationships but to some extent it could involve close friendships. Relationships involve some complex dynamics and one of the central issues in the creation or relief of stress is communication. Honest, trusting, open relationships may be the ideal but this only comes about through some commitment

8

and effort by both parties. When relationships become defined by power-plays, deceit and passive-aggressive or outright aggressive forms of communication it is a hugely stressful thing for people in, and sometimes on the margins of the relationship.

So that's my list. It could be longer but it's enough to be getting on with. One thing about the items on this list is that most point to situations and circumstances we can exert some control over, which means we aren't consigned to the role of passive victim.

Now, we react to stress in different ways of course but for the sake of brevity I can outline three. The most flexible and healthiest method of dealing with stress is through task-oriented behavior. Successful people in this regard are those who feel secure and confident. Almost invariably this level of confidence can be traced back to early life experiences where the person is encouraged to be resourceful, adjusting to the demands of the stressor, yet protecting him or herself from the mental distress. How do they manage this?

The task-oriented person seems to have the ability to weigh up a situation objectively, choose a response, and then self-monitor the reaction of their decision against the effect it is having on them. If the decision they make isn't working, they may try an alternative approach or they may make personal changes by, for example, lowering expectations, becoming less demanding and reducing their emotional investment. If none of these actions work they are less likely to press ahead and more likely to walk away from the situation entirely.

A mixture of short-term benefits, but longer-term implications, characterizes this next reaction, often referred to as defense-oriented behavior. The tension that builds from stress can be released in a number of ways. Crying, talking, hugging and seeking reassurances, are just a few examples. These forms of behavior help to relieve tension and gain sympathy from others, but if no attempt is made to address the problem(s) the implication is that the person uses defence mechanisms as a means of coping. They may, for example, deny a problem exists, embark on a series of distractive activities, or possibly regress to less mature forms of behavior where responsibilities are passed to others and they become highly dependent.

My third and final example is a process called decompensation and it represents the most seriously disruptive reaction to stress. This occurs in the face of highly stressful situations that are prolonged or demanding. Decompensation affects people at biological, psychological and behavioral levels.

The biological effects of stress involve three phases. First, there is a call to arms when the body gets prepared for fight-or-flight. Secondly, a prolonged period of resistance takes over where biological resources work at full tilt in order to try to reduce stress. Finally, when these resources are depleted, the result is disintegration and death.

Psychological effects follow a broadly similar pattern. Initial stress leads to alertness, emotional arousal and a sharpening of senses. Task-related or defensive behavior follows and here some people will cope for much longer periods than others. Mental collapse, for want of a better term, occurs as the final step in the process.

Our behavioral reaction to stress often reflects our psychological state. When stress first occurs we may reveal any number of avoidance, escape, confrontational or other behaviors in order to adapt to the situation and reduce stress. When we reach a point that nothing we try has any effect on stress reduction we reach a point of learned helplessness and therefore inactivity. Some of these features can be seen in a range of anxiety disorders such as acute stress disorder, PTSD, and adjustment disorder.

We're used to thinking about stress in terms of specific issues or circumstances. For example, exam stress, stress from noise, relationship stress and so on. This is a very practical way of thinking about stress as it helps to isolate the cause and to devise ways of dealing or coping with it. Stress is one of those words we freely throw around. Everyone has a broad appreciation of its meaning but perhaps not so many will know that there is no single approach sophisticated enough to capture and explain its actual complexity

One way to think about stress is by category. Psychologists sometimes contrast *eustress* with *distress*. Eustress (acute stress) is the call to action our bodies need when something needs to be done. As part of our survival mechanism, this form of stress represents the fight-or-flight mechanism that protects us from harm by giving us the potential to get away. Eustress is a necessary part of our arousal system but what's interesting about this type of stress is that it can feel very uncomfortable or pleasantly stimulating. For some people the point of driving fast cars, participating in competitive sports or taking a hair-raising ride at a Theme Park, is to feel the rush of an adrenaline surge. This alone tells us that stress is very much a perceptual thing. What terrifies one person gives another pleasure.

Distress, conveys the problems we experience with stress overload. If our stress system remains switched on for days and weeks at a time we reach a point where stress becomes chronic. The causes of chronic stress are varied and include living in poverty, coping with a long-term sick relative, an unhappy marriage, work-related issues and so on. Chronic stress affects the immune system and is associated with everything from cuts and grazes taking longer to heal, through to heart disease. The psychological effects of chronic stress include mood swings, depression, inability to concentrate and increased anxiety.

So far I've looked at stress mainly from the perspective of how it affects us but where stress gets awkward is in trying to explain it theoretically. There are in fact a range of perspectives on stress that derive from different theories, some of which are more accepted than others. Stress has been examined from an evolutionary perspective and this is where we get our 'fight or flight' versus 'rest and digest' ideas. The 'hourglass model' is a perspective on stress that involves a state of general physiological arousal. Here, a number of social, environmental and psychological issues feed into a common area (the bottleneck of the hourglass) and what comes through is a wide variety of possible outcomes. Other theorists focus on adaptation, some on life and health changes and some on stress as a transaction. These represent just a sample of the various approaches that attempt, or have attempted, to explain the exact nature of stress.

It may seem curious that we know so much about stress yet still find such difficulty in explaining it. In may ways this is really no different to certain disease processes where we know the effects of the disease and may even be able to treat them, but their actual cause or certain aspects of the disease, remain elusive.

- - - 000 - - -

Now lets compare anxiety with stress. Anxiety is an emotional sensation. It's the uneasy and apprehensive feeling we get when we're emotionally or physically threatened. Stress, by contrast, is often thought of as a development of situations that make us feel angry, irritated or frustrated. But stress is also a response to things like viruses, heat, cold, hunger and thirst. Stress is the way the body reacts to situations where a decision is needed, or an action, or a threat or some imbalance to its normal functioning occurs. It is a protective mechanism usually, but if constantly triggered it becomes a health issue.

If that sounds like anxiety and stress are basically similar let me provide a quick example by way of revealing some differences:

Everyone knows what a stressful day feels like. It leaves us feeling depleted, tired, and sometimes with a headache. During stress our body reacts in a certain way. It pushes out adrenaline and various stress hormones and it makes our heart work faster. This is excellent for situations in the short term but less good over long periods of time.

Any job where the meeting of deadlines is essential, or our performance is on display and being judged by others is stressful. Even more stressful is having to deal with disgruntled people, having to take on extra work, or having a boss you can't get on with. The role of long-term caregiver is also stressful, often because of the social isolation, repetitive demands and sleep disruptions that come with the role. Despite all this, we may not feel *anxious*.

Where confusion arises, I think, is we often talk about stress and anxiety *as if* they are one and the same thing, much in the way we refer to worry and anxiety. Another reason may be that people often only acknowledge they are stressed once they experience symptoms of acute anxiety. The person finds they can't concentrate as well as they used to, sleep may become disrupted and moods more tetchy and irritable. In some situations the person may develop anxiety or panic attacks.

Anxiety and stress do follow parallel paths. Independently of each other they can present a variety of health issues, yet sometimes their paths cross and coincide. As anxiety often develops from stress it is possible to reduce anxiety by reducing stress. Although it's not within the scope of this book, the good news is that a number of tried, tested and effective methods exist that allow us all to tackle either our anxiety, our stress, or both.

The Roots of Anxiety

It's no understatement to say that most people who experience clinical levels of anxiety (or depression) have had significant difficulties in their early lives. It doesn't necessarily mean that one leads to the other, and it doesn't preclude those with a secure upbringing from having these problems, but we can't help but notice the association and the way in which early life experiences often occupy a central position in affected people's memories.

In broad terms we are much more savvy about the nature of anxiety. We now recognize that childhood disorders can cast long shadows and extend into adulthood. We also know from research following people from birth into adulthood that that most young adults with a mental health problem had diagnosable problems much earlier in life. As to how early these problems start and the mechanisms that link childhood adversity and trauma to adult life, well this is more speculative. So-called adult disorders may have been set in motion during pre and/or post-natal stages of development yet for the most part our system of diagnosis places most weight on current symptoms, whilst acknowledging there may be some history.

The psychiatrist and psychoanalyst John Bowlby identified the huge importance of the parent-child relationship in the early years of life and how this goes on to influence future outcomes. Later developments in the field by Allan Schore showed how Bowlby's ideas could be proved biologically. Schore made the case that the development of an area of the brain known as the prefrontal cortex, depends on a positive emotional experience between parent and child.

The prefrontal cortex is involved with the control of pleasure, pain, anger, panic and other emotions and urges. Unlike other organs, which develop automatically, this part of the brain appears to be strongly affected by anxiety and depression. In a healthy nurturing relationship it will grow and form connections with other areas of the brain but where this is lacking the prefrontal cortex will not develop fully. Some studies of neglected babies (e.g. Eluvathingal et al, 2006) reveal they have smaller prefrontal cortexes than normal.

Fears

During the years of the great depression it was Franklin D. Roosevelt who famously commented, "the only thing we have to fear, is fear itself." The context and the timing of his remark was important. Fear is a universal emotion that varies in range, frequency and severity. It can be helpful or it can be unhelpful. We can also underestimate or overestimate our fears.

Is underestimating fear worse than overestimating it? Perhaps one is as bad as the other, but there are differences between the two. An underestimation of fear could certainly lead to situations that are really quite dangerous. For people with anxiety-related issues the situation is different. One of the common problems they experience is an overestimation of fear.

Because over-predicting fear is more pervasive it tends to be more disruptive in the everyday lives of those affected. In normal circumstances the relationship between fear and threat tend to correspond. In other words, as the threat level increases so does the fear. Fearful people react differently and this is partly due to the fact that the feared situation is usually quite harmless and commonplace.

Similar patterns of behavior are found in people who suffer from panic episodes. According to professor Stanley J. Rachman, a leading authority in anxiety and related disorders, predictions of panic tend to decrease after overestimations and tend to increase after under-predictions. Yet, predictions of future panic tend to remain unchanged whether or not a person has correctly predicted they will panic or not.

Fear is a combination of dread, physiological changes, and a strong desire to avoid or escape. It is both a reaction and a motivating force. Fear may be rational, as in behavior designed to avoid injury or trauma, or it may be irrational, as is the case in most phobias.

Normal and Generalized Anxiety

As we can't actually feel what others feel the biggest clues about our own anxiety state tends to come from other people. Perhaps they tell us that we worry too much and too often over silly little things. This really is the nub of the issue with an anxiety condition known as Generalized Anxiety Disorder (GAD). GAD sufferers worry about everything - constantly and excessively.

'What if?' questions are a real feature of GAD. These questions nearly always cluster around issues of health, family, money and work. In that regard they seem entirely normal but it is the duration and depth of concerns that distinguish GAD sufferers from what we might consider normal anxiety. These concerns also extend beyond the typical concerns of everyday life and they embrace issues of a global nature.

People with GAD are particularly sensitive to real or supposed feedback. For example, if someone at work is more efficient, or if there is the slightest hint they might have done something better, the alarm bells ring and thought processes quickly spin out of control to a point where they truly believe they are about to be fired. A husband (sufferers are usually women) who says he prefers one meal, or one dress, or one pair of shoes over another, may be seen as preparing the ground for separation or divorce. The stress of living with GAD is such that while many sufferers have little choice but to try and continue as normal a life as possible, some become too seriously affected.

At the point where normal functioning is affected a diagnosis of GAD is likely to follow, especially if problems persist for several months. By this point, symptoms of chronic worry, sleeping difficulties, a sense of dread and quite possibly a list of physical symptoms to which the person has attributed some life-threatening disease may be present.

GAD is one of the most prevalent mental health problems today. At any one time it affects around four to five percent of the population. Of these around 80 percent have some accompanying condition, like depression. As with so many other mental health issues questions surrounding its origins and development often hinge on nature versus nurture. That is, how influential are genes or the environment when it comes to understanding and treating such issues?

GAD is characterized by excessive and uncontrollable worry usually, but not necessarily, related to areas of health, finances and other minor matters that become blown out of proportion. Some people with GAD are simply unable to pin down a source of worry a feature sometimes referred to as free-floating anxiety. Before a diagnosis of GAD is reached a number of other symptoms such as irritability, sleep difficulties, muscle tension and problems with concentration also have to be evident for at least six months.

But to what extent is GAD the result of some internal psychological mechanism? The answer isn't clear but it does seem that context is important. Judith C. Baer and colleagues point out that studies of the poorest mothers show them as having the highest levels of GAD. And this, claim the authors, has nothing to do with some "internal malfunction" so much as "a reaction to severe environmental deficits".

The danger in labeling a person with something like GAD is the assumption that the cause is some internal mental state. However, in situations as reported by Baer and colleagues, it becomes clear that context is important. GAD can and does respond to treatment but if the cause is poverty then it stands to reason that "financial help and concrete services" are likely to be more appropriate.

Our Response to Anxiety

Our bodies prefer to exist in a state of balance. Even so, they are adapted to respond to the demands required of them, before returning to a state of balance. For this state of self-regulation to occur we have bodily mechanisms that speed us up and slow us down. When the so-called sympathetic nervous system kicks in we are in fight-or-flight mode and when the parasympathetic nervous system dominates we are in a state of rest-and-digest.

Our fight-or-flight mechanism enables us to cope with threats; effectively it represents our survival instinct. When a threat is sensed the fear center in the brain (the amygdala) starts a chain reaction that results in the release of the stress hormones adrenaline, noradrenaline and cortisol. These hormones make the heart beat faster, divert blood to muscles and increase levels of glucose in the blood to act as an energy reserve. The air passages dilate to allow more oxygen to be taken in and digestion slows as energy is diverted for other needs.

Unfortunately our fight-or-flight capabilities are somewhat lessened in modern living. Instead, we find ourselves subjected to all the stressors that activate the sympathetic nervous system but with outlets that rarely involve fight-or-flight. When the sympathetic nervous system kicks in it can leave us with some fairly unpleasant physical sensations to deal with including:

- Palpitations and chest pains.

- Sweating.
- Dizziness.
- Dry mouth.
- Trembling.
- Tingling.
- Muscle tension and stomach cramps.
- Feeling faint and sometimes feelings of unreality.
- Nausea.
- Urge to urinate.
- Tightness in the throat and difficulty swallowing.

Anxiety sometimes extends to everyday living and the very dramatic sensations associated with fight-or-flight are much less pronounced.

Our Response to Stress

Well, I've said it's down to fight-or-flight, but does this explanation work as well for women as it seems to for men? Not necessarily, according to research conducted over the past decade. Before I address this it might be helpful to provide some perspective and take a step back in time.

In the 1920s Walter Cannon first described the "acute stress response" and the way our nervous system and hormones respond when we perceive a state of threat. What this boils down to is the greater our perception of threat, the more intense and prolonged our physical reaction will be to it. In order to dispel the threat we're left with two basic choices – deal with it (fight)or get away from it (flight).

Since then our understanding of the stress response has become more refined, but it is still based largely on the basic principle of fight-or-flight. A question asked more recently is, how well do these early principles stack up with what we know about women?

Professor Shelley Taylor and colleagues decided to look at things differently. From their perspective, women are considered less likely to benefit from fight-or-flight, especially if they have babies or young children. They also reasoned that females of different species tend to form tight, stable alliances, which might suggest a greater need to seek out supportive relationships. The scene set, the team embarked on a program of research that examined diverse cultures as well as everything from studies on rats to primates. What transpired has developed into the first new model of stress for decades.

The "tend and befriend" model is not an alternative to fight-or-flight. Indeed the authors point out that the initial shock response in terms of hormonal and nervous system activity is much the same for women as it is for men. However, other factors can intervene to make fight-or-flight less likely in women. Aggression in men, they argue, is more likely to be regulated hormonally. In women, if aggression does occur, it is more likely to be defined by circumstances and confined to specific situations that require defense. Similarly, immediate flight during times of danger would put offspring at risk.

Taylor and colleagues suggest these gender differences are related in part to hormonal differences. Oxytocin, for example, promotes caregiving and underpins attachment. Under stress, some mothers appear to increase care and nurturing behaviors, suggesting an increase in oxytocin levels and there is evidence that females prefer to seek out the company of others, especially other females. Making use of social support networks appears much less of a priority for males. What is equally evident is the fact that men do use social networks for a whole variety of reasons.

Until fairly recently the assumed wisdom has always been that men tend to retreat into themselves during periods of stress and that very often this is accompanied by higher risk behaviours such as gambling, smoking, drinking, unsafe sex and drug use. Given that the tend-and-befriend model was only articulated in the late 1990s it seems logical to refocus the spotlight on men.

A team of neuroscientists and psychologists at the University of Freiburg has overturned some long held assumptions about male isolation and its association with stress. The research team developed a public speaking task in order to induce stress. Specially designed social interaction games were then introduced, the aim of which was to measure positive social behaviours like trust and sharing as well as negative behaviours. The male volunteers under stress acted more positively than those not under pressure, while negative social behaviour was unaffected by stress. The team went on to report that positive social contact with a trusted individual before a stressful situation reduces the stress response as much as during or immediately after a stressful event.

This suggests that the male emotional and behavioral reserves may run deeper than previously assumed. Greater male flexibility is good news and could suggest useful points for intervention. Stress, it now appears can tease out men's gentler sides. The higher men's heart rates and cortisol levels, the more trusting and friendly they became. Tend and befriend, it appears, is not exclusive to women.

Alcohol

Humans have been brewing up and consuming alcohol in some form or another for thousands of years. It's safe to say very many of us enjoy and some even seem to require its psychoactive properties. Today it is a comparatively inexpensive commodity and we're spoilt for choice as to flavors, strengths and novelty value. As a drug, we have embraced it more fully than anything else. It is legal, it is interwoven with social and business-related activities and it is frequently used in times of celebration. But it is also used as a means of self-medication and it's this to which my post now focuses.

After a busy or stressful day it's a common enough practice to meet with friends at the bar or go home and pour a drink. There's nothing wrong with this course but if the motive for drinking is to reduce stress on a regular, i.e. daily basis, then problems are beginning to stack up. Part of the problem lies with the fact that alcohol is an addictive drug and as with all addictive drugs more is required over the longer term in order to achieve the desired effect. So, in a typical scenario of low mood, stress, irritation or anger, the downing of a glass of alcohol can make our problems recede in a fairly rapid and pleasant fashion. Symptoms of stress and anxiety can literally disappear in minutes.

It's easy to see why so many people with anxiety-related issues find a drink of alcohol is so appealing. In fact anxiety sufferers are around three times more likely to turn to alcohol or some other form of substance abuse. What many may not realize is just how short-lived an effect it is. Every time alcohol leaves your system your symptoms become just a touch worse, over time it becomes more tempting and more necessary to open another bottle, or to refill your glass. Anxiety levels slowly begin to rise and alcohol is not far behind. This is the start of alcohol dependency and a vicious cycle.

What starts off as an easy and effective way to provide temporary relief from anxiety can lead to a point where alcohol itself is inducing anxiety. There are several other outcomes of self-medicating with alcohol and none of them are good. Alcohol is a toxin, so your mental and physical faculties will be negatively affected. Attempts to withdraw from consuming alcohol can itself cause anxiety because you are effectively attempting to remove yourself from an addictive substance. In battling both withdrawal symptoms and increased anxiety the temptation to drink more alcohol increases.

Drugs and alcohol tend represent a short cut to pleasure or release and a way of feeling the burdens of life recede into the distance. It's an illusion of course and once the effects wear off the problems still remain. The relationship between alcohol, drugs, depression and anxiety states is strong. Most studies estimate 20-30 percent of people with depression, bipolar, or anxiety disorders misuse alcohol or are alcohol dependent. So what's happening and why?

Let's first consider the direction of the relationship. Is it drugs and alcohol that cause anxiety disorders or depression in the first place? Well, they may be strong contributors but survey results also suggest that in more than two-thirds of women who suffer from depression and who are alcoholics it was the onset of major depression that *preceded* their drink problem. In men the results are different, where one-fifth of cases appear to experience major depression prior to becoming alcoholics. But of course not all users of alcohol are technically alcoholics.

Alcohol is easy to obtain and relatively cheap. For people with anxiety disorders and depression it is most often used as a form of self-medication. As users will attest, when the short-lived effects wear off, even deeper depression is experienced. The temptation then is to take more. But, as with so many drugs, people develop a tolerance to alcohol over time. It means more has to be consumed to get the same effect and damage to the body starts to increase.

Drugs can alter brain function. We know this from scans that show decreased activity in the frontal lobes. Decision-making is then affected and even the experience of joy becomes blunted.

We know that in some cases the treatment of the addiction, whether drugs or alcohol, is sufficient to lift depression. For alcoholics with depression it is the combination of medication and regular and accessible social support that appears most effective.

Depression can and does arise from abuse of alcohol or drugs. The reasons people become dependent in the first place varies, but issues of low self esteem and confidence, ease of availability, peer pressure, low social and work prospects can all contribute. The recreational drug ecstasy is suspected of causing long- term damage to the serotonin system, which in turn is involved in the regulation of emotions and the onset of depression.

Depressed drinkers start to feel better within weeks of cutting out alcohol. The usual process is to tackle the alcohol first and deal with the depression second if it hasn't resolved after a few weeks. Either way, some help, support and direction may be needed. Your family doctor can provide this, or get advice from self-help groups such as Alcoholics Anonymous

The message for longer-term anxiety sufferers is very simple. Don't use alcohol as a means to control your anxiety. Of all the possible alternatives in the treatment of anxiety, alcohol is probably the worst and the most damaging and will certainly never provide a solution.

Anger

How do you think of your anger? Are you quick to flare up and then do you quickly cool off? Does it take a lot to get you annoyed before you boil over and simmer for days? Do you bite your lip only to find your stomach churns with the strain of it all? We all have our ways and we all have different triggers. Some things, for example, set the fuses alight and they fizz away in the background. Other things seem to bypass all the filters and *boom* we erupt. Now when I say erupt, I don't necessarily mean tipping into a rage. You may be the sort who internalizes your anger. The basic mechanism for anger and the way we react are different things. But it's helpful to know a few things about both.

People who are prone to anxiety and stress generally find they start to take things more personally and they feel hurt as a result. It can lead to false interpretations of passing comments or the behavior of others, and a tendency to overlook positive things in preference to focusing on the negatives. Collectively, this constitutes what is known as a negative thinking style. It can also lead to black and white thinking. For example 'those I trust and those I don't', 'people who are useful and those who are useless'. Ideas become polarized and there seems little scope for a balanced way of thinking.

Angry people sometimes have unhelpful beliefs about their anger. Some may argue it is inherited therefore there is nothing they can do about it. Others may believe their anger stops others from walking all over them. A common belief is that controlling anger is bad for you and that it should be released or something worse (often unspecified) may occur. It's helpful to apply a little logic here. We *all* have the capacity to be angry but if this extends into all areas of life there's a problem.

We can begin controlling anger by tackling its various components. These include reducing the associated physical symptoms, finding ways to control angry behavior and changing our mindset to accept anger triggers as problems to be solved rather than a personal attack that requires a pre-emptive or retaliatory strike.

We have all experienced anger and we know the causes are many and varied. Moods boil over as a result of some real or perceived injustice, or a stress or frustration too many. When anger becomes too strong, occurs too often or leads to aggression and violence it affects others. We know this, and many of us know that anger is one of the diagnostic features of mood disorders such as generalized anxiety disorder (GAD) and depression, yet surprisingly little is known about the anger-mood disorder relationship.

The consequences of anger are nearly always negative. People who experience a lot of anger also put their own health at increased risk. Coronary heart disease, raised blood pressure, diabetes and bulimic behaviors are just a handful of health problems to be associated with anger. But it also appears that anger and anxiety are partners. Recent studies have shown that heightened levels of anxiety are uniquely related to GAD and that internalized anger – boiling inside without showing it – is a stronger predictor of GAD than other forms of anger .

Quite why anger and anxiety tend to co-exist isn't clear. Sonja Deschênes, author of the previously mentioned GAD study, suggests that anxious individuals tend to assume the worst and that outcomes that could be either good or bad present a kind of ambiguity that increases anxiety. Exactly the same process appears to occur in people who are easily angered which leads her to suggest anger and GAD may be two manifestations of the same thought process.

One of the great myths, sadly promoted in too much self-help literature, is that letting rip with anger can be a good thing. Anger is never helpful and its expression means there is a danger of losing control. There is a big difference between assertion and anger. Anger negatively affects the way we feel, think and behave and, as mentioned, has only negative health implications.

Burnout and Rust-Out

Jack was a high achiever. He was full of enthusiasm and energy about his work. He'd willingly put in the hours and more besides. He'd worry about standards, defend his work, extol its virtues and he felt part of something bigger than himself. Then somewhere along the line all this began to change. At first Jack put it down to feeling a bit tired and a little out of sorts. But these new feelings and thoughts slowly took up residence. Increasingly he began to question the worth of what he was doing and the fact that his hard work seemed to be taken for granted. Jack found it easier to stand back and see the cracks in the system. His thoughts and his comments have become increasingly cynical. Jack notices how he's become detached, tired and irritated by the tasks he has to accomplish. In short, Jack has all the symptoms of burnout.

The psychologist, Herbert J. Freudenberger, is generally credited with coining the term burnout and defining it as, 'the extinction of motivation or incentive, especially where one's devotion to a cause or relationship fails to produce the desired results.' The sense of trying harder while seeming to achieve less is a central feature of burnout.

It was Freudenberger who also commented upon the sense of 'omnipotence' that frequently accompanies someone in the situation of burnout. Even if offered, they are likely to refuse help from other people in the belief that only they have the capabilities for the job. This, despite the fact that their work may have become sloppy, and behind schedule.

The physical and emotional exhaustion associated with burnout can manifest itself in terms of suspicion of other people's motives, depression and an increase in psychosomatic symptoms such as headache, backache, difficulty sleeping and stomach complaints. As such the person becomes more irritable, inflexible, critical, and reluctant to view themselves as having a problem. Yet, if ignored, the situation simply worsens.

More enlightened companies recognize that burnout is commonly associated with people in positions of authority who have simply worked too hard for too long. Some even have established systems for recognizing and working with individuals or groups who either suffer from or are at risk from burnout.

There is another side to the coin. Imagine you're involved in a job that is unrewarding, repetitive and just plain boring. You feel restless, unhappy, stuck in a rut. You find yourself grumbling to co-workers, friends and family. This is called rust-out.

Rust-out is the term occupational psychologists give to symptoms arising from jobs that leave people feeling apathetic, disinterested and dull. Effectively it's the opposite of burnout yet some of the effects appear remarkably similar. Productivity slows, mistakes increase and quality suffers, at least this in jobs where such things can be seen or measured. Other jobs are mind-numbing, simple and repetitive, and it may be harder to spot rust-out except perhaps from increased sickness and absence.

The common factor with burnout and rust-out is stress. With burnout there is simply too much stress but with rust-out there isn't enough positive stress to keep the person interested. Regular and sustained levels of boredom are actually highly stressful.

Many previously complex jobs have been unpicked within systems that involve less hierarchical structures. This has a couple of effects. The first is that opportunities for promotion become more limited resulting in often well qualified and highly motivated young people working in jobs where there is little or no scope for advancement and undertaking tasks that are unfulfilling and sometimes demeaning of their capabilities. Secondly, older people in more middle-management posts who find themselves unable to advance, simply find themselves going through the motions and counting off the days until they can retire.

The problem can be tackled from two directions. First, any employee who feels themselves underwhelmed by work can consider varying their own activities or approaching their employer to request new responsibilities. If, as is possibly the case, these simply don't exist the only real course of action left is to seek different employment.

A second possible direction for change is for managers to become more aware of the likelihood of rust-out in their organization. They might, for example, vary or rotate tasks in order to maintain interest. They might take the time to match employees to the correct level of job and to spot talent that might be languishing in some easily overlooked places. Involving employees in new projects, testing ideas and decision-making, helps them feel valued and useful.

Positive Burnout

More and more we hear of high achievers, people at the very top of their game, who simply pack it all in and walk away. Is it possible just to fall out of love with success and achievement, or are other factors at play?

There are a lot of high achievers in the world and probably many more who would like to be. The quest for success probably starts at a very young age and from that point a considerable amount of effort and energy is applied in order to get to the top. Alongside the drive for achievement is the stress of envying and competing with others. Many people who succumb to depression are high achievers, unable to stop pushing themselves, yet increasingly aware of their dysfunctional and unhappy lives.

We tend to measure success in material ways and through the acquisition and flaunting of objects. For some people this is enough but it isn't uncommon to find that the acquisition of 'stuff', and sometimes power, isn't as fulfilling as it may have appeared on the way to the top. Typically, sacrifices to fulfilling and honest friendships have been made and rivalry and destructive competition dominates over nurturing and fulfilling relationships.

Kate Losse joined Facebook in its early days. Her experiences and her decision to quit are articulated in her book The Boy Kings: a journey into the heart of the social network. Losse reveals how her, "initial enthusiasm quickly submerged by tedium", and how "I was relieved at lunchtime when I could walk out of the office to San Francisco's long piers." She refers to "a form of crisis. You think you're working your way up, but, really, you're just servicing someone else's vision and it's making you disappear. I was using all my intelligence to cope with the fact that I was in an environment that had nothing to do with who I was. So I left."

Having the insight and courage to walk away is far from admitting defeat. Almost invariably it leads to something simpler, less stressful but more fulfilling, more satisfying and importantly, more rounded and grounded in terms of lifestyle and relationships.

Body

Appearances matter, but for 1 in 100 people they seem to matter too much. Excessive worry about some minor or imagined issue with appearance is called body dysmorphic disorder (BDD) and it has become a common mental health problem.

We begin to pay more attention to our appearance during adolescence, so it's not surprising to learn that problems often start during this sensitive time. A lot of time may be spent gazing into the mirror, comparing appearance with friends and celebrities and feeling self-conscious about blemishes, physical development, and facial characteristics. All of this is perfectly normal and most people manage to grow into their skin and accept things for what they are.

For others the situation is more complex. They become distressed and anxious about some perceived physical defect which others find way out of proportion. The focus of attention often relates to one or more features of the face but other parts of the body may also be involved. A great deal of time may be spent checking the mirror and using make up in attempts to hide or diminish the perceived problem. In more extreme cases people may avoid social contact, be unable to establish relationships, or maintain employment. They believe people are staring, talking or laughing about their situation, but this simply isn't the case.

BDD is more common in people who suffer with social phobia, generalized anxiety disorder or depression. It also occurs alongside eating disorders and obsessive-compulsive disorder (OCD). It is a highly distressing condition associated with very high levels of suicidal thoughts and suicide attempts. One investigation published in the Journal of Clinical Psychiatry, found 78 percent of sufferers experienced lifetime suicidal ideation (thoughts about suicide) and 27.5 percent had made suicide attempts. In fact completed suicide rates may be more than double those of clinical depression and 45 times higher than that of the general United States population, according to Phillips and Menard (2006).

The cause or causes of BDD are not fully understood with explanations ranging from genetic predisposition, to neurotransmitter imbalances in the brain, to physical or emotional neglect. Some similarities exist between OCD and BDD although current thinking suggests the conditions are different. People with BDD often repeatedly check their appearance in the mirror, can't relax unless they have removed and re-applied make up, or positioned hair so that it helps to cover a perceived problem.

The top five concerns of BDD sufferers are skin, hair, nose, weight and stomach. Cosmetic surgery may appear a likely solution to solve some of the problems but research conducted in 2010 by Katherine Phillips, MD, found only two percent of procedures reduced BDD severity. In a survey of 265 cosmetic surgeons, 178 (65 percent) reported treating patients with BDD, yet only one percent of the cases resulted in BDD symptom improvement.

Brain

Many of our moods depend on our nervous system. Too much or too little of the chemicals that speed things up or slow things down and the whole thing can go out of kilter. The basis of many of our anxiety medications is to correct these imbalances. To form an appreciation of the issue I've outlined just five of these essential neurotransmitters and the way they work:

Glutamate and GABA can be thought of as mainstay neurotransmitters. They slog away in high concentrations within the brain where glutamate is the throttle and GABA acts as the brake. Glutamate has an important role in learning and memory but too much and it can lead to agitation, impulsive behavior and even violence. GABA has the opposite effect. It increases our levels of tranquility by inhibiting too much nerve activity. Some of the most frequently used drugs for anxiety aim to enhance the action of GABA.

Increasing Your GABA Levels Naturally

Physical activity encourages the development of neurons in an area of the brain called the hippocampus, a portion of which is associated with processing emotions. Some of these new neurons are young and excitable but others are designed to release GABA. Elizabeth Gould, director of the Gould Laboratory at Princeton University, has demonstrated that regular exercise encourages GABA release during stressful situations which encourages more rapid recovery.

Psychologist Dr. Mike Dow makes various dietary suggestions some of which relate to GABA. Oolong tea, cherry tomatoes, kefir (a probiotic drink) and shrimp are some of the examples he offers, but they represent just part of a well balanced diet that requires reduction in fatty, processed and sugary foods.

I mention exercise and diet because these two areas offer rather more compelling evidence in relation to mood. The fact that a connection between mood and GABA is established has resulted in some sections of the food supplement industry to make bold claims about its effects. In fact the evidence supporting the use of commercial GABA supplements for mood states is very thin indeed, so do think carefully before parting with your cash on GABA supplements.

Dopamine is our arousal and stimulation neurotransmitter. We associate dopamine with rewards as it controls our appetite for sex, eating, pleasure and even creative thinking. Too little dopamine can lead to depression but too much can lead to dependence on the agent doing the stimulating. Cocaine, for example, increases dopamine levels in the brain's reward circuit and, for a period, can produce intense pleasure. Long-term use seems to result in neural degeneration from overproduction of dopamine.

Endorphins are both hormones and neurotransmitters and they can pack a punch. We have at least 20 different types of endorphin some of which are more powerful than morphine. We release endorphins when we're under stress or in pain. The higher the level of endorphin the less pain we feel and the more relaxed, even euphoric, we can become.

There is some speculation that a lack of endorphins could explain anxiety-related conditions such as obsessive-compulsive disorder or even clinical depression. Endorphin deficiency disorder (EDS) may be genetic or acquired and the associated symptoms are very similar to clinical depression or bipolar disorder. Acquired EDS tends to be of shorter duration and can result from inadequate exercise, pain, or emotional stress.

Increasing Your Endorphins Naturally

Intense exercise can result in the so-called runners high. Well that's one way to it, but if you'd prefer a less taxing alternative try something like tai chi or meditation. A *light* intake of alcohol also stimulates endorphins as do foods like chocolate and chili peppers. Ultraviolet light also gets those endorphins moving, so get out and about during the day.

Noradrenaline (norepinephrine) is the main neurotransmitter of the sympathetic nervous system. We associate this with our fight-or-flight mechanism and moderation of other physical actions such as heart rate and blood pressure. Too little noradrenaline and we become sleepy and lethargic. Too much and our thoughts run away with us, we become twitchy and nervous, our hands and feet go cold and our blood pressure climbs.

In the case of persistent anxiety our own ability to produce a natural chemical substance called dynorphin may be influential. Dynorphin is produced in the brain and spinal cord. Chemically, it has broadly similar properties to opiates such as opium and morphine, although chemical studies suggest it is at least six times more powerful. Our bodies appear to produce different types of dynorphin and these are involved in regulating emotion, motivation, our experience of pain and how we respond to stress.

Various studies show that the level of dynorphin in our bodies can have dramatically different effects. In some situations dynorphins can produce feelings of euphoria but in others can stimulate pain rather than relieving it. Some studies show that blocking dynorphin can reduce depression, yet high levels are linked with resistance to cocaine addiction, overeating and hyperthermia.

Andras Bilkei Gorzo and colleagues from the Universities of Bonn and Berlin, say if the brain produces too little dynorphin symptoms of anxiety will not subside. In one stress experiment, volunteers with lower gene activity for dynorphin were compared with those with higher activity. During the experiment volunteers wore computer glasses and were subjected variously to the appearance of blue and green squares. When green squares appeared an unpleasant stimulus to the back of the hand was applied using a laser. Stress reactions were observed by measuring increased sweat on the skin.

As part of the experiment brain scans were taken. These revealed that volunteers in the low dynorphin group showed stress reactions for considerably longer than those in the high dynorphin group. The amygdala, an area of the brain that processes emotional content, was also shown to remain active for longer in the low dynorphin group.

The study suggests that *forgetting* anxiety is an active process that involves different parts of the brain. Volunteers in the low dynorphin group appeared to have less 'coupling' of these areas, which could explain why they retain the memory and anxiety associated with trauma for much longer.

Breakdowns

When I was young the term 'nervous breakdown' was still very much in use. It was really a general term used to explain things that weren't physical in nature but that somehow conveyed the person was no longer able to cope with things the way they were. These days we talk more about stress-related disorders.

In real terms nerves don't break down at all and neither has there ever been a formal diagnosis of nervous breakdown. Even so, people still talk about 'their nerves' as a focus for stress or anxiety. So why is the idea of our nerves so compelling and where did it all start?

Medical historians point to the 19th century as a key period in the development of ideas about the mind and body. It was a time when the medical profession embraced mental disorders as sickness and the body was often likened to a machine. Mental disorders were often considered to result from some weakness or failure of the nervous system. Dr. George Beard used the term neurasthenia in 1829 to describe symptoms such as fatigue, dizziness, depression and anxiety, which he attributed to depleted reserves of energy in the nervous system. It was thought that the condition arose when people, particularly women, had taken on more than they could cope with but that following a resulting illness the person would normally recover.

Neurasthenia became a popular idea and its causes were considered to relate to rapid industrialization, poor and cramped housing conditions and disease. The most common treatment was rest and fresh air. Beard and others went on to experiment with a variety of electrical 'treatments', some of which were taken up by the private clinics and sanatoriums of the day.

The diagnosis of neurasthenia remained popular into the 20th century, its use gradually fading into the 1920s as greater inroads into medicine and psychiatry were being made. Perhaps its not so surprising that we hang on to the idea of nerves to explain stress-related disorders. We all know what people mean when they say they are 'nervous' or perhaps have a 'nervous condition'. These terms have found their way into our everyday language much in the way that engineering terms like breaking point, stress and tension are used to describe certain psychological processes. We also know that while nerves don't break down, the action of medication for the treatment of anxiety or stress is specifically designed to have some effect on the neurotransmitters.

A few decades ago the idea of the nervous breakdown was something that often made people – well, nervous. As with so many mental health issues it was a dark, mysterious, feared, embarrassing and misunderstood concept. These days I'd like to feel we've made a few positive inroads into mental health issues and things slowly but surely are starting to improve.

Children

Slowly but surely we are coming to realize that many of the same mental health problems that plague adults also affect children. It used to be considered that children were too immature, both physically and emotionally, to experience issues like anxiety or depression. The tendency was, and often still remains, to brush over childhood concerns as a passing phase – the natural bumps and psychological grazes we all incur as a result of growing up. It's clear however that many adult problems are laid down in childhood and whilst parents may acknowledge this they may still wonder whether their approach to childhood anxiety is helpful.

When I mention brushing over concerns but I don't mean to imply that parents are insensitive to anxieties, merely that the typical response is along the lines of offering bland reassurances, much in the way our own parents or other adults did to us. In the case of repeated anxieties, such as going to school, being bullied, etc., the 'it'll pass,' or 'everything will fine,' approach can send a message that you don't really understand. For a child the emotions are mixed. Yes, you've given them attention and you show you care but there may also be a niggling feeling of being misunderstood, which can be hurtful and isolating.

In much the way a therapist might approach adult anxieties it may be more helpful to allow your child to fully discuss their feelings and then move towards evaluating the pro's and con's of different courses of action. In other words rather than telling the child what to do and how to do it, see if you can encourage them to come up with options. Of course depending on the age of the child you may need to help shape some ideas or discourage one's that are inappropriate.

As much as we may want our children to be happy and active the fact remains that children develop and express themselves in ways that may be puzzling to adults. Showing curiosity is no bad thing. For example, when you see a child looking puzzled or unsettled, ask why as you might an adult. If you see them playing alone when they normally wouldn't, wonder why. Over time it's good to explore emotions together. Children often don't have the words to explain their feelings so toys can help. Some children project feelings onto a favorite doll or object, for example.

Bullying and Its Consequences

Sleep-related problems such as nightmares, sleep walking and night terrors are known collectively as parasomnias. The relationship between anxiety and parasomnias in young people is associated with bullying.

As more and more is being understood about the effects of bullying it becomes clear that the longer bullying lasts the greater its effect on the long-term health of the victim. All schools have some form of bullying policy but the degree to which it is enforced or is effective probably varies greatly.

When researchers from Boston Children's Hospital examined the issue they discovered that bullying at any age is associated with worse mental and physical health, increased symptoms of depression, and low self-worth. Chronic bullying makes matters worse, with victims reporting increased difficulties with physical functions such as walking, running or sports-related activities.

Bullying also casts a long shadow. Even at the age of 50, children who were bullied at school are more likely to have poorer physical and psychological health and cognitive function. According to research undertaken by King's College London, and published in the American Journal of Psychiatry, frequent bullying at school is associated with an increased risk of anxiety disorders, depression and suicidal thoughts. Social relationships also suffer with bully victims less likely to be in a relationship, to have good social support and enjoy a higher quality of life satisfaction.

But back to an earlier stage in life where it is reported that children who are bullied at ages 8-10 are more likely to suffer with parasomnias. Previous studies also show that being female, having persistent sleep problems and emotional problems in childhood increases the chances of parasomnias.

Bullying is often hidden although its ramifications may be clearer to see. Anxiety, disruptive behavior or withdrawn behavior are clues. If the child is also experiencing parasomnias then this may indicate the child is being bullied and should be investigated.

City Living

The number of people living in cities continues to grow. Some estimates are that around 70 percent of people are likely to live in cities by the year 2050. City living provides a rich, stimulating, social and cultural environment as well as easy access to medical care and a range of other facilities. The down side is that the risk of suffering from anxiety disorders is 21 percent higher than those who live in more rural settings and 39 percent higher for mood disorders.

Findings from an international research study published in *Nature* demonstrate that certain regions of the brain involved with emotion regulation and stress are sensitive to the experience of city living. Using a series of MRI scanning experiments, researchers compared the effects of an induced stress task to volunteers from both rural and urban areas. Those living in urban areas showed much higher stress responses. Dr. Jens Pruessner of the Douglas Mental Health University Institute in Quebec, who helped run the study, also said the incidence of schizophrenia is almost doubled for individuals born and brought up in cities. It isn't yet clear why these areas of the brain are more active in city dwellers but possible candidates for consideration are toxins, crowding and noise.

One reason why some people appear to thrive in cities whilst others yearn to leave may be the degree of perceived control individuals have over their daily lives. Plus of course cities tend to have higher rates of crime and certain areas that are more no-go than others. Then again, city's can be lonely places. An environment of high social density coupled with social isolation and real or perceived vulnerability can hit some people hard.

The possible effects of city living are increasingly under investigation. Traffic and aircraft noise, air and light pollution, over-stimulation, shift work, unemployment, crowding, lack of green spaces, are just a few of the issues under scrutiny.

We can't however assume from this that all city living is bad. Cities tend to provide rich culture, easier access and greater variety to services such as healthcare and education, and standards of living may also be generally higher. Some have well established and supportive communities. It's perhaps more of a trade off between those of us at high or low risk of mental health problems and the circumstances we find ourselves in that may matter the most.

Dental Phobia

Some common questions around dental anxiety revolve around whether the person suffers with anxiety or phobia. In fact the gap between anxiety and phobia is somewhat blurred. Typically, a phobia is considered an irrational fear that leads to avoidance or escape. So by that definition all those people who worry about their appointment but manage to haul themselves to the dentist aren't really phobic, although they may feel highly anxious.

The reasonableness or otherwise of anxiety varies from person to person. If you're in my 50+ age bracket you will probably remember times when dentistry was not without its painful moments. In fact your anxiety about visits to the dentist probably still revolves around the prospect of pain. It's only a couple of years ago that I had a wisdom tooth removed and despite sitting calmly in the waiting room I can assure you my pulse rate was anything but calm. In many respects dental surgery is no different to any other form of surgery. People naturally feel anxious in the run up to treatment and feel relieved when it's over. However perhaps you have a genuine terror of dental treatments or examinations?

Dental phobia isn't just about the fear of pain. It often involves deep-seated control issues in which we have no say or control over the procedure, the time it takes, or when something might cause discomfort. We may fear the dental examination room itself, the lights, the noise of pumps and drills, the way dentists are dressed and masked. We may fear the intrusion of things into the mouth, or choking, or of being sick, or just the proximity of the dentist and their assistant to our face during a procedure.

Of course if fear of the dentist keeps people away there's a problem brewing. The chances of dental decay and gum disease increase and with this general health can be affected. Rotten teeth are not nice to see or to have. They can increase anxiety, affect self-esteem and the longer the situation goes on, the more embarrassing and difficult it becomes.

Increasingly, dental practices put time and resources aside to treat dental phobia. They work at the pace of their patient and will address any fears the person may have. Dental phobia is highly responsive to treatment and many dental surgeons are trained and highly skilled in helping patients overcome their fears.

Other Medical Anxieties

Medical procedures vary greatly as to the extent of intrusiveness and complexity. Despite this even the simplest procedures may generate high levels of anxiety in some people. Unfamiliar surroundings and smells, strange people speaking in jargon and lack of understanding as to what is happening and why are just some of the reasons people feel under stress.

Some medical procedures require little more than offering a tablet. Some are painful, some intimate, some difficult and lengthy. Many will leave the patient with little or no control over what is happening to them. As patients, the way we cope with such situations depends on a variety of factors. Previous experience and knowledge can make a big difference, although in some situations a little knowledge may be almost as bad as too much. Generally though our age, gender and the social and cultural context to which we are familiar has a big influence over how well we are prepared to take action in order to reduce anxiety.

Some early studies into the needs and expectations of patients were simple but interesting. Typically both patients and health professionals would be asked to rank a list of things felt to be most or least important to patients during a stay in hospital. It was quickly discovered that the priority lists for patients were in stark contrast to those assumed by health professionals. A lot has been learned since then, most notably the fact that the patient's perspectives should have priority when it comes to helping them cope with anxiety in the order and at the speed they require.

Helping people cope with the anxiety of medical procedures is a two-way street. The health professional needs to know the type of information that is necessary and that will be of benefit, but they need to tailor this to the needs and capabilities of the individual.

For the benefit of argument let's assume the patient is about to undergo some surgical procedure, although it could just as well be a course of radiotherapy or say ECT for depression. Five broadly overlapping types of information will be of benefit. The first of these is simple factual information about the procedure(s) and what will happen. The second is how this will make the person feel in terms of their senses. For example, they may want to know that it is perfectly normal to feel sick following anaesthetic. The third relates to any particular emotions that may be evoked and the fourth a time frame for recovery. Although not strictly related to the procedure it is important for the patient to know how long they may be out of action as a result of their condition.

With all of these issues, effective communication is the key to helping reduce anxiety. Not all patients like to ask questions and not all know what questions to ask. It shouldn't be assumed that silence equates to satisfaction. Neither should it be assumed that having imparted information it has been remembered or understood. Even the most relaxed and intelligent person can find themselves overwhelmed with information and terminology. As much as information can help to reduce anxiety it must be remembered that anxiety also serves to block information. For this reason, time, careful use of language and checking that information is understood are essential skills for caregivers in helping patients cope with anxiety.

Differences

I've used a number of terms in the book. I've reminded myself this is an A-Z for beginners and whilst I don't want to state the obvious or appear patronising I also don't want to assume we're all on the same page. This chapter is about differences. So many anxiety concepts overlap that it can be tricky to follow what's going on. Therefore I'm listing just a few of the most commonly recurring themes in anxiety in order to illuminate what's what:

How Do Anxiety, Panic and Phobias Differ?

What's common to all three and what's different? Common to all are the causes. It appears that any of these conditions can run in families and this points to inherited risk factors. Most experts believe the relationship between genes and environment is important. Our life experiences and circumstances can make us more vulnerable to the onset of any of these conditions. Our own behavior can also increase the risk of onset. For example certain drugs, alcohol or even caffeine can trigger the conditions.

But there are differences. Panic is a sudden and often unexpected rush of anxiety. The focus for the person affected is their body and health. A phobia is a fear of a situation or object and anxiety is the sense of feeling worried, tired, irritable, and being unable to focus. Note a key difference between this and panic is that the focus of attention is not usually related to health or illness – unless there is a very specific reason.

Anxiety and panic are strongly related to depression, whereas phobia usually isn't.

When it comes to treating anxiety, panic or phobia, there are several options that can be useful for all. Medications can help to take the edge off and sometimes antidepressants are prescribed. Some people find that beta-blockers help to reduce the physical side (tremors, shakiness, heart thumping) of anxiety related conditions.

Self-help is an option for all these issues, but if they are accompanied by depression it may be better to seek professional advice, unless you feel your depression is quite mild. There is no shortage of self-help books relating to anxiety, panic and phobias and many DVDs and CDs based on cognitive therapy can readily be found.

Talk-therapies are another option that can suit all conditions. These may be individual or group oriented sessions. Voluntary self-help groups are often more informal but they can be very supportive in terms of the understanding people will have of your situation and useful coping strategies they may be using. Some may be facilitated by a health professional but this isn't always the case.

How is Stress Different to Emotional Trauma?

We have sophisticated survival mechanisms to help protect ourselves from physical danger. Once we sense harm the body responds by releasing adrenaline, cortisol and other hormones. We may not perceive getting caught in traffic, being late for work, or being a caregiver as threatening, but the body does. This means stress reactions occur in some form, for most of us, a great deal of the time and as emotional trauma is included in the mix one question to ask is, what's the difference between stress and trauma?

Let's take a relationship breakdown as a common example. Most people would agree that such an event is a distressing and highly stressful experience, but for some the experience can be traumatizing. Like stress, it seems that our emotional reaction to a circumstance is the key. What is stressful to one person isn't necessarily the same for another. Similarly, it is the individual's experience of an event that determines whether they find it stressful or traumatizing.

There are thought to be three key ingredients to emotional trauma. First, the person is completely unprepared for the event. Secondly, nothing the person could say or do would have any effect on the event occurring. Thirdly, it was completely unexpected. What tends to make this different from 'normal' stress is the intensity of the experience, the length of time it lasts and the time it takes for the person to settle. Unlike stress, it may be harder or impossible for the person to talk about their experience. In effect the intensity of the experience is such that it becomes locked in, sometimes to the point where the person isn't even aware of the effect it is having.

The effects of trauma may not appear for months or even years later. Even the more commonplace symptoms are complex and may not be recognized for what they are. They include changes in sleep and eating patterns, sexual dysfunctions; psychological issues such as depression, mood changes, anger, lapses in memory, flashbacks and guilt. Relationships may also suffer and a pattern of self-destructive behavior may emerge.

The way we think about emotional trauma has changed a lot. It is no longer associated as an outcome of major catastrophes and is now recognized as an intensely personal reaction that hinges upon individual history, coping skills, the meaning the event has for that person and the extent of support and reactions from friends, family and relevant professionals.

How Do Men and Women React Under Stress?

It's an issue that continues to exercise the brains of academics. Women, for example, are argued to find less benefit from fight-or-flight than men. The reason, argue professor Shelley Taylor and colleagues, is that women's priorities tend to differ. Fight-or-flight isn't always helpful if babies and young children are involved, so women try to adjust to circumstances and form tight socially supportive networks, a model now being referred to as Tend-and-Befriend.

Little by little we're finding out more about gender differences. In 2011, Nichole Lighthall, a USC doctoral student, reported her findings that men and women react differently to risky decision-making, and this is reflected in different brain activity patterns according to gender. When not under stress, she says, men and women appear to think in similar ways. Under a stress simulation task men appear to have a higher drive to act quickly whereas women tend to slow down. Women appear to become more cautious over decisions and strive to make the right choice. Men's performance on the task was much better however and they appeared more motivated towards achieving smaller rewards.

Stress appears to undermine empathic abilities in men but increases them in women. I can almost hear the chorus of, 'no surprises there.' Men under stress tend to turn inward. They become more self-centered and less able to distinguish their own emotions and intentions from those of other people. As men become more stressed they seem less able to take on the perspectives of those around them and are much more inclined towards egocentric actions.

Women seem to apply more social strategies when under stress, according to research published in the journal *Psychoneuroendocrinology*, by Giorgia Silani and colleagues. At a psychological level women may have internalized the knowledge that they receive more external support when they interact with others. The more stressed they are, the more they apply social strategies.

Social Anxiety or Social Phobia: What's the Difference?

Jake is 30 years of age. He's had a couple of girlfriends but nothing that really lasted too long. Whenever an attractive girl speaks to Jake he feels self-conscious. He struggles to find things to say, stumbles over his words and blushes. It's easier and less embarrassing for him to make his excuses and walk away.

Sue is articulate and intelligent but outside of her immediate family she keeps people at a social distance. Sue is actually concerned that if she let's people get too close they will see through her – and not like what they see. She feels sad about her situation but she has also become very adept at keeping a low profile and avoiding attention

Jake and Sue are experiencing what is known as a social phobia. A social phobia is really an extension of social anxieties that most of us have experienced at some point in our lives. So when does social anxiety become a phobia? The fact that the lives of both Jake and Sue are affected is a prominent feature. If we could speak to Jake or Sue we'd also learn they worry a lot about doing or saying something embarrassing and that they feel others are judging them. It makes them feel worried, self-conscious and inadequate.

Social anxiety is so common that sometimes the distinction between it and a phobia is hard to determine. For people with the more extreme forms of social anxiety there is an implication for treatment; this being that no form of treatment can ever get rid of social anxiety. So, the aims of treatment focus on helping people feel less distressed and preventing anxiety disrupting their lives.

Social anxiety and social phobia seems to affect men and women equally. Shyness is certainly a recognized feature of childhood and social anxiety is perhaps just an extension or more extreme version of this. By the time we reach adolescence our level of self-consciousness can be quite high. As adults we can see social anxiety manifest itself in various forms. During a social encounter some people chatter away nervously and then calm down, others are more reserved and like to take stock before they warm up. We've seen them all, the outgoing, the exotic, the shy-and-retiring, the frosty and judgmental, the cynical, and so on. Many of these social mechanisms are put forward as a defence or a way in which we'd like to see ourselves portrayed.

Disorders

We categorize the symptoms of anxiety according to certain specific features and this tends to affect the way we approach and treat them. There is however considerable overlap in the symptoms of the anxiety disorders and this is because the most common feature of them all is anxiety.

If we look across the board, that is, from phobias, panic, GAD, OCD, health anxiety and Post-Traumatic Stress Disorder (PTSD), eight symptoms are characteristic of them all:

Avoidance: anything that makes us feel uncomfortable tends to be something to try and avoid. This fight-or-flight mechanism kicks in when we encounter situations or objects that cause anxiety arousal.

Physical arousal: is all part of fight-or-flight. The body switches into its action settings and as a result we feel the associated sensations of increased pulse and breathing rates, tingling in the hands and feet and sweating. If our anxiety is very pronounced we can experience difficulties in breathing, knots in the stomach, nausea, dizziness and even visual disturbances.

Intrusive thoughts: these are constant reminders of the issues that cause anxiety and embarrassment. In most anxiety disorders they lead to a kind of predictive anxiety, where the person is certain they won't cope. In OCD the thoughts can be highly distressing.

Vigilance: people with anxiety are often highly tuned to their environment and become very alert to circumstances that may cause them to feel anxious or may threaten their escape or avoidance of anxiety provoking situations.

Safety seeking: people with anxiety often adopt behaviors that help them cope. They may, for example, never go out unless they are with a partner. They may avoid eye contact to reduce the chance of social interaction or they may ask a lot of questions in order to avoid focus on themselves. These may provide temporary relief but they are a constant reminder to the person that the situation is unsafe and they have to do something to cope with it.

Threat estimation: two of the most common features of anxiety are the over-estimation of threat and the under-estimation of being able to cope.

Worry: even when away from situations that provoke anxiety, the anxious person may spend a lot of time reflecting on and worrying about past and future situations. Typically various 'what if' scenarios occupy their thoughts.

Low mood: anxiety can be an exhausting thing to live with. Anxiety and depression are commonly related but even if the symptoms of depression are sub-clinical, the person with anxiety will often experience low moods because they feel drained of confidence and see no particular relief in the future.

Acute Stress Disorder

Vehicle collisions, rape, natural disasters and armed conflicts. These are just a few examples of the many unexpected and unwelcome traumas that can affect people for years. We cope with traumatic experiences in very different ways and while some people appear able to adapt and move on, others have greater difficulty. A particular group of symptoms, characterized by a state of inner distancing from the trauma, has become known as acute stress disorder (ASD). Of central concern to some experts is the fact that those who show symptoms of ASD are more likely to develop chronic post-traumatic stress disorder.

The symptoms of ASD include a reduced sense of awareness of surroundings and a feeling of numbness or detachment from the event or situation. The person believes the circumstances around them aren't real (de-realization) and they frequently refer to their feelings as being like they were in a dream. Sometimes there is a sense of being outside of the situation, like an observer looking in, but not actually being involved. It is as though the person is floating above or around the situation but their body is in a different place altogether (depersonalization).

When asked to recall particular features of the trauma, the sense of dissociation sometimes extends into memory. This seems to be some kind of protective mechanism where very significant aspects of the trauma become locked down. This form of localized amnesia is however a reversible condition.

People with ASD symptoms effectively show early signs of post-traumatic stress disorder and for this reason some experts question whether it is a unique condition in its own right. For a diagnosis of ASD to be made the aforementioned symptoms must be present, but also a minimum of one symptom associated with PTSD. For example flashbacks of trauma, an active avoidance of reminders, and thirdly, increased vigilance, sleep disturbance, irritability, poor concentration and an exaggerated startle response.

As with most psychiatric diagnoses, there is a requirement that clinical distress extends beyond personal discomfort and in some way actively disrupts normal social and/or work functions. Further examples include aggressive or suicidal behaviour, self-harm and sexual dysfunction. Symptoms must last for a minimum of two days and a maximum of four weeks, and must occur within four weeks of the trauma.

I've mentioned that the emotional effects of highly stressful events may vary from person to person. Even so, reactions tend to fall into one of three general categories although sometimes there are elements of overlap:

The initial shock that sometimes follows a stressful event is often referred to as an acute stress reaction. Physical symptoms may include nausea, chest pain, rapid heart rate and difficulty breathing. Acute stress reaction may start immediately or possibly a few minutes following the event. People suffering acute stress reaction may feel dazed, confused and as though they are detached from reality, but other symptoms such as anxiety, anger, irritability and wanting to be left alone are also common.

Very often, the person recovers fairly quickly but sometimes they do not. If the disturbances associated with an acute stress disorder lasts for a minimum of two days and a maximum of four weeks, and have occurred within four weeks of the traumatic event, a diagnosis of acute stress *disorder* may be considered. For this to be diagnosed however, the problems must cause clinically significant distress or impairment in social, occupational, or other important areas of functioning or impair the individual's ability to pursue some necessary task, such as obtaining necessary assistance.

Adjustment reaction is the term used to describe psychological symptoms that start following a stressful event such as the termination of a relationship, the collapse of a business, a robbery, etc. Symptoms occur within one month of the stressful event, and frequently tend to resolve within six months. They may include marked levels of distress, possibly out of proportion to what might normally be expected. Depression, anxiety, irritability and a sense of being unable to cope are features, although adjustment disorders are also diagnosed according to specific symptoms i.e., adjustment disorder with anxiety, with depression, with disturbance of conduct, and others beside.

Post-traumatic stress disorder (PTSD) also follows a stressful event but tends to come on weeks or even months later. The nature of the event is likely to be quite traumatic and probably very threatening. Although PTSD is often associated with military conflicts it can actually follow any kind of serious incident such as a violent attack, a natural disaster, or even witnessing incidents like a train crash or serious traffic accident. PTSD can occur at any age and persist for years. Symptoms include flashbacks of the incident, nightmares and intense distress with anything associated (sights, sounds, smells) with the trauma. In addition, sufferers often experience generalized anxiety, panic, depression, guilt, hypervigilance, irritability and anger and blunting of their emotions.

Eating

We are regularly bombarded by messages about food, its effects and what is good and bad for us. Just when you think you've grasped these ideas they seem to change again. The messages can also seem contradictory. We know that too many sweet or fatty things help to pile on the pounds, yet there's an image in front of us of a slim bikini-clad model gorging on a chocolate covered ice cream.

Is there an adult out there who hasn't been on a diet of some sort? Well, of course there is, but plenty more of us find ourselves standing on the scales and wondering where all the extra pounds have come from. Then there are the diet fads. Come on, what have you tried? The boiled egg diet, perhaps? Maybe you were a fan of the Atkins diet, or the South Beach, or Grapefruit diets? Losing a few pounds when you're overweight is a good thing, although as most people know some dietary fads were too extreme to be healthy. Keeping a check on weight is one thing but some people get so anxious about their weight, shape and diet that it starts to really affect their life. If this happens it's called an eating disorder.

Eating disorders are known to affect men and women but the causes seem to vary. Certainly we're more aware of ideal type images and the ways in which these can strongly influence people. We also know that eating anxieties tend to start during teens and early twenties. This may be due to any number of stressful issues such as exams, or coming to terms with bodily changes and sexuality, or unrealistic expectations about shape and weight, and more besides.

Self-esteem issues are often bound up with eating disorders. Childhood abuse, the death of a close friend or relative, other traumas such as sexual, physical or psychological abuse are just some examples where negative emotions are generated and may lead to eating disorders.

Food can also become a way of exerting personal control. This can happen when people feel they will be happier (I'll be more attractive and better liked) or punished (I'll make myself sick) or as a means of distraction. Distraction is sometimes used in situations of parental conflict where a child provides something for parents to worry about instead of arguing. The anxiety for the child is that if they put weight back on the conflicts will begin again.

Health

In many ways everything in this book relates in some way to health and wellbeing but I'm including this chapter because it specifically directs attention to what is happening to us either directly or indirectly as a result of anxiety and stress.

People who are vulnerable to anxiety tend to go through a particular set of routines when they enter a potentially intimidating situation. Rather like tuning a radio, they scan rapidly and broadly in order to identify possible threats. These potential threats are then tuned into and the volume is turned up in terms of their heightened state of arousal. The whole process involves a psychological interpretation of events but it also feeds into, and feeds off, changes in the body.

When something is appraised as potentially threatening a part of the nervous system, called the sympathetic nervous system, kicks in. A rush of adrenaline and noradrenaline floods the body. The heart rate quickens, sweating increases and pupils dilate. The body is ready for fight or flight, which is designed to reduce or prevent the perceived threat. Everyone is aware of these effects to some extent, but changes in the body don't necessarily stop. Many of these we are completely unaware of, including the influence they may have on health.

An anxiety provoking moment triggers something called the hypothalamic-pituitary-adrenocortical (HPA) system. The HPA produces a number of substances but the most important is cortisol. It is the combined effect of continued activation of the sympathetic nervous system and HPA activity that may have serious consequences for health.

Professor Jane Ogden, a health psychologist at the University of Surrey in the UK, states that prolonged production of adrenalin and noradrenalin can result in irregular heart beats, increased heart rate and blood pressure, increased risk of blood clot formation, fatty deposits and plaques and suppression of the immune system. The body becomes more prone to infection and the risk of heart and kidney disease increases. Prolonged HPA activation also appears to decrease immune function and leads to damage in a region of the brain known as the hippocampus. Over time, psychological issues such as loss of memory, loss of concentration and psychiatric problems may appear.

Other important factors have to be accounted for when considering the link between stress and illness. Stress is often a trigger for additional activities that have a direct effect on health. The most obvious of these are smoking, drinking alcohol, changes to diet and less exercise.

A variety of medical conditions are strongly associated with anxiety. Moreover, any drug that affects the sympathetic nervous system is also a candidate for anxiety symptoms (for example asthma inhalers or nasal decongestants). Here are some examples

Hyperthyroidism, is a condition where the thyroid gland is overactive, can lead to anxiety. This is the most common of the endocrine diseases occurring most commonly in women between the ages 20 - 40. Symptoms include a fine tremor, irritability, restlessness, insomnia, excitability, nervousness, sweating, palpitations and persistent fear and worry.

Mental health symptoms are often some of the early signs of under-active thyroid with up to 12 percent of cases reporting anxiety, poor memory, speech deficits and diminished learning capacity. Some estimates suggest between 30 - 40 percent of people with hypothyroidism have an anxiety disorder. Once treatment commences anxiety symptoms tend to subside anywhere from days to months later.

Chronic breathing disorders such as asthma or emphysema are often associated with anxiety. This is explained by the inability of the person to breathe effectively. Low blood sugar, not necessarily associated with diabetes, can result in anxiety. This can occur in cases where the person is working hard and has overlooked a meal. Other medical conditions where anxiety may be a feature include:

- Obesity
- Irritable Bowel Syndrome
- Fibromyalgia
- Super-ventricular arrhythmias
- Ventricular arrhythmias
- Migraine
- Chronic Obstructive Pulmonary Disease
- Tumors of the Adrenal Gland
-

Health Anxiety

When a person experiences persistently high levels of anxiety, usually for six months or longer, and the focus of this anxiety is on their own or a loved one's health, they may be suffering from something termed health anxiety. A feature of health anxiety is that it often exists in the face of evidence that suggests nothing is wrong. So how does it develop in the first place?

Current thinking tends to point to one of three possibilities, although to some extent these may overlap and support one another. The first relates to our own development. Imagine growing up in a household where chronic pain or illness is a central issue. In such a context it's easy to see how illness can be regarded as something permanent, disabling, painful and possibly even progressive and degenerative. Watching adults struggle with daily living isn't an easy thing for a child or adolescent to cope with and could, so the argument goes, contribute to how we learn to view and respond to illness.

A second possibility is genetic vulnerability. Various lines of research continue to explore the relationship between anxiety (not just health anxiety) and genes. Genetic mapping certainly points to associations between genes and anxiety. In other words it seems quite reasonable to suggest that we are born with greater or lesser sensitivity to things that make people anxious. Of course our personality and our environment could influence the way genetic vulnerability actually affects us.

Thirdly, we should consider the effect of the internet and the media generally. We generally like to consider ourselves astute enough to understand the way the media works but its influence is still profound. Media outlets often tend towards the sensationalizing of stories. These stories grab our attention and they tap our vulnerabilities. If we add the influence of the internet it's possible to see how anxieties can develop. The term cyberchondriac is sometimes used to describe the person who seeks medical information on the web. The results of one Microsoft study pointed out that search engines can't discriminate between minor or major symptoms. The search term 'headache' is as likely to uncover material on stress, as it is meningitis or brain tumors.

Cyberchondriasis

Since medical knowledge became freely available to anyone with an internet connection, the urge to seek out answers to symptoms has increased. The term cyberchondria, the internet 'equivalent' to hypochondria, reflects the fact that roughly two percent of all internet searches are health-related, with around a third of people escalating their search in order to investigate serious illnesses.

Hypochondriasis refers to imagined diseases or conditions that cause significant anxiety and distress to the sufferer. The condition tends to develop in people around their mid 20s to 30s and appears equally distributed between men and women. If left unchecked, the condition can develop into an all-consuming obsession, in which normal bodily sensations are taken to be symptoms of terrible diseases.

So, are you a "cyberchondriac"? According to Arthur Barsky, MD, author of *Worried Sick: Our Troubled Quest for Wellness* (1988), illness is central to the identity of the hypochondriac. If you find yourself latching on to serious illnesses that frequently have ambiguous symptoms such as lethargy, flu-like symptoms, headaches, and so on, you could be something of a cyberchondriac.

The problem for cyberchondriacs, or people heading in that direction, is that they frequently focus on reputable medical websites. This leads to a furthering of anxieties as they find symptoms that appear to match their own. Health anxieties are thought to cost billions of dollars each year in unnecessary tests and sometimes treatments.

Signs and Symptoms of Health Anxiety

Most of us have concerns about staying healthy but fortunately we aren't preoccupied to the extent it gets in the way of our everyday lives. Some people however worry a great deal about their health and no amount of reassurance seems to last for very long.

Health anxiety affects how people think, feel and behave. The most obvious symptoms are worrying about health when there is no medical reason and seeking reassurance from people around you that everything is fine. Some people with health anxiety spend a lot of time reading, listening to or watching programs about health and illness. Others may spend time examining their body, worrying about little bumps and bruises and noticing bodily sensations.

The sensations of health anxiety are pretty universal. Those affected feel worried, tense, tired and unwell, as well as woozy and detached. Feelings of dread may bubble up and the person feels unsettled and edgy. Thought processes involve worries that symptoms might not be taken seriously and that something may have been missed. There is often a feeling that something might be very wrong and that if this is ignored it will only get worse. The most common health concerns range from a general sense of being unwell through to thoughts of cancer, brain tumors, or the signs of a heart attack or stroke.

As worries build the anxious person will make repeat visits to their doctor, often with a new symptom they hope may finally shed some light on their condition. They will behave in ways that shows they feel ill and this isn't difficult because the health anxious person their symptoms appear to support their illness. Physical sensations include headaches, sweating, dizziness, aches and pains, changes in breathing and tingling and muscular tension.

There is no one cause for health anxieties but we know it often becomes more extreme around times of high stress. For people who experience health anxiety most of the time we know there are a few things that seem to maintain the problem. There is an unusual focus on physical sensations so the more they focus the more heightened the sensation. This is often accompanied by mirror checking, prodding and squeezing of certain parts of the body. Unhelpful thoughts further underpin the problem, as they tend to be catastrophic in nature. A headache is seen as a symptom of a brain tumor, cancer or a stroke. Death or paralysis is bound to follow and the children will be left without a parent. Another habit that develops is the seeking of reassurance from others. It keeps symptoms in the mind and increases the chances of other people asking how they are feeling.

All these signs and symptoms probably say something about deep-rooted and possibly unrealistic beliefs relating to health, illness, vulnerability and negative thinking.

Coping with Health Anxiety

If you've found yourself associating with the material on health anxiety, this section may be useful. There are some very good reasons to curb concerns over health. Just think of the time you may already have spent fretting over health matters. Any kind of attention given to some sensation or action tends to exaggerate it. The same is true of pain and even skills that seem very familiar. Ever watched a professional golfer miss a hole they were just inches away from? It's partly a problem of over-thinking and of being over-concerned.

So far as health is concerned one place to start is to keep a record (nothing fancy, just a piece of paper) of how many times in a day you seek reassurance. If you do this over a few days you'll have a measure of the problem and something to compare to when you take action. The action is very simple. All you need to do is make a conscious effort to reduce the number of times you seek reassurance. You'll find that this may increase your anxiety in the short term but will actually reduce it over the longer term.

Distraction is a very good technique. People tend to worry more when their mind is occupied on other things. The busier you are the greater relief you will experience.

Body checks, such as prodding, squeezing, or looking in the mirror are very common. If this sounds familiar adopt a similar strategy of counting the number of times you self-check and then make a concerted effort to reduce that number.

The biggest problem is finding ways to stop worrying. You can't stay busy all the time but you can try to stop the things that fuel your concerns. Stop reading medical stories, watching them on television, listening about them on the radio or searching for things on the internet. Ask your family and friends to support you. Try to replace health worrying thoughts with more balanced thoughts. It won't change overnight, but when a worry comes into your head make an effort to counter it with an alternative

Now consider all the things you've been avoiding because of worries about health. Reintroduce yourself to them – one at a time if it helps, or make a plan to remind yourself of the things you've been avoiding and then list them in the order you'd like to pick up on them.

Stress and Ill Health

The negative effects of stress can be seen both physically and psychologically. In this post I want to focus on just seven of the physical conditions either known or generally regarded to have stress as a primary or related cause.

High blood pressure can occur if adrenaline levels remain high. When blood vessels narrow they constrict the blood supply to various organs and this has consequences. Restriction of blood to the kidneys, for example, leads to the production of a hormone that increases blood pressure further. The liver meanwhile produces more cholesterol and other fats that merely collects in blood vessels if not used up.

Gastric upsets in the form of inflammation or possibly ulcers occur as a result of stomach acid production. Long term the muscles around the bowel may spasm leading to painful irregular bowel movements, constipation and diarrhea, a condition known as irritable bowel syndrome.

The immune system is affected because the stress hormone cortisol has anti-inflammatory properties. This is good for dealing with injuries but it also has the effect of down-regulating the immune system. The long-term result of this is we become more vulnerable to infections.

Cancer, or rather some cancers, also seems to be influenced by stress. It's not uncommon to find cancer cells in the body but a robust immune system deals with this as a matter of course. Chronic stress may lead to a higher incidence of stress and for people who have cancer it seems stress influences tolerance to treatment and recovery.

Muscle tension. Stress manifests itself through anything from jaw tightening, teeth clamping and frowning, to hunched shoulders, neck and backache. It can result in anything from headaches to repetitive strain injury. It's good therefore to consciously relax your muscles a few times a day and give your body a good shake down.

Sex hormones are affected by stress. Anyone suffering from stress knows how it interferes with his or her sex drive. In men it may influence the ability to achieve or maintain an erection. In women, periods may become irregular or lost altogether.

Type 2 diabetes isn't something you might have associated with stress but here's how it works. Raised levels of cortisol result in an increase of fats and glucose into the bloodstream. The pancreas responds by producing more insulin to try and control glucose levels. Over time the liver builds a resistance to insulin and sugar builds up in the blood and tissues. This is type 2 diabetes, a form of diabetes that is avoidable, and is associated with an unhealthy lifestyle.

Hormones

When the body is under a state of stress it responds by producing stress hormones. Then, once the stressful event has passed, the body begins the process of breaking down the excess levels. The neurotransmitters GABA and serotonin help to get rid of stress hormones like cortisol and adrenaline and, over time, the body and mind become more tranquil. If however we continue to be stressed our bodies respond by continually attempting to produce stress hormones.

The body can only release adrenaline for so long before levels start to deplete. When this happens we begin to feel tired, emotionally fatigued and inattentive. Continued demands on our adrenaline can raise blood pressure and increases the risk of coronary heart disease. This alone is cause for concern but experts in the field of stress have mainly focused their attention on what has become know as the stress hormone - cortisol.

Cortisol isn't just produced as a result of stress. This naturally occurring hormone has a variety of important functions such as maintaining the water balance of the body, stimulating the release of endorphins and helping to relieve inflammation. Ongoing high levels of cortisol are a different matter altogether. Cortisol in excess is known to damage neurons in an area of the brain involved in emotion and memory. Too much cortisol also negatively affects the immune system and this leaves the person vulnerable to disease and less able to repair damaged tissue. It can also affect sleep patterns by stimulating the body when it should be asleep.

Chronic stress can have the effect of depleting the body's supply of noradrenaline. An excess of cortisol and adrenaline goes on to impede normal brain and memory functions. There are a variety of physical and psychological consequences. Physically, the risk of cardiac disease increases, but a range of other problems including endocrine, metabolic and gastro-intestinal disorders can result. Psychologically, the sense of helplessness and despair associated with chronic stress can lead to severe depression.

Hypervigilance

From everything you've read so far it will be clear that anxiety is not a single event. It is a process that involves various components embracing both the activation and experience of anxiety.

People vary in their proneness to anxiety but a person who is vulnerable is also hypervigilant to their surroundings, especially if the situation is new, relatively unfamiliar, or potentially intimidating. Try the following questions:

1. Do you experience difficulty getting to sleep at night?
2. Do you find yourself waking up during the night?
3. Could you easily fall to sleep in a public place, like an airport, or on a busy train?
4. Do you find strangers easy company?
5. Do you prefer not to have people stand or sit behind you?

If you answered yes to most or all of these questions it would suggest that you are hypervigilant, and this makes perfect sense in the context of anxiety. Here's another example:

Jason is a tall, athletic and physically fit 15 year old, who is being bullied at school. To avoid the bully he hangs back from the school gate until the last possible minute. When he moves from class to class he checks the corridors, moves rapidly, and makes a point never to loiter. If he sees the bully he goes rigid. He feels his throat tighten and panic starts to set in. Even though the place he needs to be is just a few feet away he will either hide until the coast is clear or take the much longer route in order to avoid any contact.

The process of hypervigilance typically involves a rapid scan of the environment, which then narrows to a highly focused level of attention if a potential threat is spotted. Whatever the threat is (a person, a social situation, an object) it rapidly takes on a sharper and more defined quality and signals a change in behavior. The person may find a reason to escape or avoid the threat, or if this is not possible may remain in a state of high arousal and attentiveness in which coping behaviours, often involving seeking something or someone to hold on to, may result.

Hypervigilance is characterized by increased physical and psychological arousal. Physical sensations, as mentioned previously, will typically include sweating, increased heart rate and rapid shallow breathing. Emotional concerns may lead to a whole variety of behaviours designed to help make the person feel more secure. For example, carrying a weapon for fear of assault, or avoiding situations where people sit behind them, or being sensitive to sounds during the night and lying awake as a result.

Not surprisingly, hypervigilance is considered a common feature of various anxiety disorders, including PTSD. In some cases it can be extreme enough for the person to become almost entirely preoccupied with scanning their environment for threats. They may become agitated in crowded or noisy places and may adopt a number of obsessive behavior patterns as ways of coping.

Language

A person who suffers with anxiety will often keep a lid on the way they truly feel. It may not take much to get them talking but what results can leave the listener confused as to what is really being said. We all have our own vocabulary. These are words and common phrases that help in the crafting of our identities. How we use these words and phrases often reflects our emotional state.

If we want others to understand how we feel about something there may be the temptation to exaggerate in order to convey the gravity or intensity of an event or situation. Yet if we are in the role of *listener* and actively attend to what is being said these words may cluster and they can tell us about the key issue of concern. Here are some examples:

Let's imagine you're listening to a friend who uses words like *conflicted, trapped, undecided, pulled apart or bewildered* in their conversation. Well, these are all examples of confusion and they reveal something about the way your friend is feeling.

Words such as *uneasy, worried, nervous, panicky or tense* are examples of fearfulness.

When talk includes words like *distressed, hurt, lonely, miserable or drained* then sadness or possibly depression may be the key issue.

Anxiety talk reflects any number of emotions but if we hear words like *furious, resentful, uptight, bitter or disappointed* then anger is certainly a feature.

We can contrast these with words like *eager, excited, content, calm or glad* all of which we tend to associate with happiness.

So, what are we supposed to do we listen to anxiety language? Saying 'you sound a bit upset' may be sympathetic but it's also pretty vague and states the obvious. Actually being able to condense words into categories can be helpful and anxiety levels can sometimes reduce as a result of feelings being identified for what they are. If I hear someone relate sadness talk, I can tactfully bring the conversation to a point where I might be able to get them to talk about that sadness.

Our use of language tends to provide signals as to the way we truly feel about something, yet feel incapable of pinning down. By identifying the root issues it then becomes possible to consider alternatives and leave behind a vicious cycle of thinking and inertia. Remember, an anxious person isn't necessarily using language in a measured or tactful way. They are expressing emotions and if they've bottled up emotions they can sometimes come at you like a broadside. But, when the person calms down and talks about things in a bit more detail, you can often get to the nub of the problem.

Memories

Nothing improves memory more than trying to forget. It's an old saying with more than a grain of truth. Yet the more often we trigger a memory the greater the chance some minor change takes place. Memory feeds imagination and is fairly easily distorted. Remember going back to your old school? How the rooms seem so different now? Minor distortions in memory usually do us no harm but they often reveal differences in the ways a shared event was perceived. You look back fondly on an event, for example, only to find the person who was with you pointing out you didn't see it that way at the time. That tells us memory is also selective and can even be prone to change depending on our mood at the time of recall.

Our memories are laid down in different places within the brain. The sights, sounds, times and place of memories are all stored in different regions. However, each memory has an emotional element and the area of brain that stores this emotional memory is called the amygdala. Our worst memories tend to be those with a strong emotional component. These are the times when we said or did something that makes us cringe with embarrassment. They may be times when we ourselves were snubbed or suffered some kind of rejection. These are painful experiences but emotional pain matters when in comes to developing coping strategies.

Everyone has memories they'd like to forget but fortunately most people have one's they cherish, look back on fondly or that make them laugh. It may seem odd to talk about our 'relationship' with personal memories but the connection between memories, and our emotional reactions to them, appears to influence our levels of anxiety.

We all have different way of regulating our emotions and the way our emotional memories affect us is shaped by our personalities our gender and the strategies we use to regulate our emotions. We know, for example, that people who score highly on neuroticism tend to focus on negative emotions when they are under stress. If this continues, they are also more likely to develop anxiety-related problems and possibly become ill with depression.

Some studies have begun to look at the strategies people use to regulate emotions when they recall positive or negative memories. For example, some people may exaggerate or focus mainly on the negatives while others are inclined towards putting a more positive spin on unpleasant memories – a process referred to as reappraisal.

In 2012, Ekaterina Denkova and colleagues of the University of Illinois at Urbana-Champaign, published results of their study in the journal *Emotion*. They found that those who used reappraisal when recalling negative memories were more likely to recall positive aspects. Men who attempted to suppress negative emotions were as likely to recall positive as negative memories. Where women were concerned, suppression of negative memories was significantly associated with lower moods afterwards.

The use of reappraisal therefore is associated with less social anxiety and less anxiety in general than those who avoid expressing their emotions. Even we need to be wary of over-optimism as this too can have its problems. For example, it may incline people to believe they are unlikely to contract illnesses or diseases if they don't take suitable cautionary measures. Similarly, there are many times when keeping a lid on emotions is appropriate as a short-term strategy.

There are however some memories that are so traumatic, so destructive and painful that it's hard to see any merit in them. People suffering with PTSD are haunted by such memories, to the point where their daily lives are affected. We tend to think of soldiers or perhaps victims of some terrible natural disaster as those likely to suffer from PTSD, but trauma may also extend from childhood and symptoms masked by physical complaints, depression, and/or anxiety, all of which can lead to difficulties in diagnosing PTSD.

Professor Karim Nader, a neuroscientist at McGill University in Montreal, is one scientist to have reported significant clinical improvements in people suffering with PTSD who have taken propranolol. Nader suggests that the beta-blocker drug is effective because it disrupts the process of memory storage once the memory is activated. Normally, he says, the brain uses proteins to restore memory but propranolol seems to have the effect of disrupting and possibly even erasing the negative emotional components associated with traumatic memories. In the next experimental phase, scientists plan to target the amygdala area of the brain. They will ask PTSD sufferers to verbally recall their experiences in as much detail as they can. If successful, propranolol will disrupt the subsequent storage of recovered memories so they will fade or even perhaps be forgotten. And, if the drug therapy is eventually adopted, it is likely to be structured around something like cognitive behavioral therapy.

Midlife

By the time people reach their midlife it often becomes increasingly clear what their career limitations are. They find it harder to change career or even to slide across to other companies in the same or similar roles. There's also a good chance they are in a position of some responsibility, along with all the stress that comes with the job. Looking forward to retirement, or even early retirement, may seem a way to leave all the stress behind, but is it really that simple?

It's now both proven and accepted that long-term stress has damaging effects on our health, yet the effects of stress into old age are just beginning surface. Depending on the type of survey conducted, estimates of perceived work-related stress vary anywhere from 30 to nearly 60 percent of the working population at any given time. Over the past few years, research into mild or moderate work-stress during middle age, shows an increased likelihood of disability in old age.

In 2011 results from a study from the Gerontology Research Center in Finland, involving the follow-up of 5,000 adult workers for 30 years, found those who reported long-term stress at work were more disabled during retirement. Stress symptoms including sleep disturbances, physical problems and negative reactions to work were tracked in workers aged 44 to 58 years of age. Those with the highest stress symptoms were 2-3 times less likely to be able to walk two kilometers, had greater difficulties with dressing, bathing, shopping, housework, taking medication and using the telephone. Dr. Jenni Kulmala, lead author of the study, suggests that chronic activation of stress responses results in "wear and tear" of the body and increases the risk of old age disability.

Similar findings, published in 2011 in the *Journal of Epidemiology and Community Health*, tracked 17,000 working adults between 2002 and 2007. During this period 649 people started receiving some form of disability benefit – 203 for a mental health problem. Those with the highest levels of stress at the start of the study had a significantly higher chance of being awarded disability status. However, even those people with mild stress were 70 percent more likely to receive benefits.

Poor work ability in midlife predicts earlier death and disability in old age, found Finnish researchers. In another 2011 study, this time following 6,000 white and blue-collar workers over a 28-year follow-up, the risk of early death was found to be highest in blue-collar workers, although white-collar workers followed a broadly similar gradient.

How should be consider such findings? Certainly there seems to be a case for suggesting the demands placed on people in some occupations exceeds their ability to cope. Increasingly this is becoming a feature of modern day living where the focus is primarily on work while the nurturing of supportive networks and close relationships are pushed into second place. At what point do we take stock of this and recognize the insidious effects of stress beyond the point of a working life?

Money

Most people know what it is to feel a financial squeeze but debt can be something of a low blow, coming as it sometimes does with redundancy, job loss or changes to working hours. The stress comes from any number of places. If you have savings, they may begin to deplete at an alarming rate. You may turn to credit even though you don't have the means to pay it back. Perhaps you are scraping by but things are so tight there's nothing left for emergencies or even little treats? You feel a failure because you're letting yourself down and maybe even the people who depend on you financially.

With all these negatives it isn't surprising to feel your confidence is taking a beating. You wonder what it is that you've done to deserve this and yet no matter where you turn nothing seems to improve. So you begin to look inwards. There seems nothing to get up for so you stay in bed and you rationalize this because your sleep pattern is poor and you feel generally unwell. You talk yourself down, believing you'll never get another job or that things will never improve. In other words you're feeling anxious and depressed.

It's very common for people in difficult financial situations to go through a bad patch, after which they dust themselves off and try to move forward. It's the moving forward that can present the biggest challenge, especially where debt is concerned, so what might help?

If you find your mood is hampering progress and nothing has improved after a few weeks it might be useful to pay a visit to your doctor and report your symptoms. There are however some self-help techniques to consider.

Try to get back into some routine. If you've lost your job this is especially important. Take stock of your situation as it affects you today. Very often people worry about the future and when this happens everything becomes amplified and gets out of control.

Get in contact with your credit providers and explain your situation. They will invariably work with you to negotiate either a break in payments, or a revised payment schedule to help you through the worst patch.

Seek advice from others. You aren't the first or last person to experience money problems so use services like Citizens Advice who in turn may suggest other sources of financial help or other forms of support.

While this is happening it is helpful to address the stress. Get some exercise, remind yourself that you are dealing with the situation, avoid alcohol, try to eat healthily and restore your sleep pattern.

OCD

Obsessive-compulsive disorder (OCD) can be considered a disorder of brain and behavior involving obsessions (intrusive negative thoughts that won't go away) and compulsions (the irresistible urge to behave in certain ways, often repeatedly). OCD is classified as an anxiety disorder.

No one factor seems to account for the disorder. OCD sometimes runs in families and stressful events can account for onset in around one in three cases. The neurotransmitter serotonin may have a role in OCD as studies have shown brain imbalances of serotonin. Some people have especially high standards of personal morality, which may or may not embrace a religious faith. Concerns over certain thoughts can have the effect of heightening awareness of them and greater difficulties in shaking them off. It used to be thought that parenting style was influential in the development of OCD. There is some evidence that overprotective parenting can increase the risk of developing OCD but on the whole upbringing is not considered to be a factor.

Estimates suggest that one in 50 people will develop OCD. It generally starts during teen years but not everyone seeks help, or they put off seeking help, sometimes for many years. Statistics from The National Institute of Mental Health point to equal numbers of men and women being affected and that approximately 2.2 million American adults have the disorder.

Most people with OCD have both obsessions and compulsions but it is estimated that as many as 20 percent have obsessions only and 10 percent have compulsions only.

Some Examples of Obsessions

At the outset it is worth pointing out that a hallmark of OCD is that the person recognizes their excessive thoughts and behaviors are senseless. Obsessive thoughts can actually cover any subject but in general they fall into one or more of five categories. These include:

Relationships e.g. doubts over faithfulness, needs for reassurance.
Sexual thoughts e.g. fears of becoming attracted to family members, people of the same sex, touching children inappropriately.
Magical thoughts i.e. the mere thought of something could make it happen.
Religious thoughts e.g. having bad thoughts in a place of worship, sexual thoughts involving saints, God or other religious figures, fear of swearing during an act of worship.
Violent thoughts e.g. harming a loved one, self-harm, acting on some violent impulse.

Obsessional Thinking

Obsessional thinking is a real personal battle. The person understands the lack of logic behind their thinking and they understand that their thought processes are of their own design, but they also feel it is a process out of their control. Obsessional thinking tends to defy rational thought processes and anxiety increases as a result.

Obsessional thoughts are unpleasant, unwelcome and repetitive. Common themes include harm being inflicted on other people, often close to them, sex, contamination from bacteria and viruses and bad language. Obsessive thoughts may also include the fear of making mistakes or behaving in some inappropriate way. There are some well known obsessions, mainly due to the fact that the obsession (the thought process) frequently translates into a compulsion (some action). They include concerns over security (locked doors, gas turned off, light switches) and the need for exactness and arranging things in order or sequence.

Thought-action fusion is the term usually applied to a particular feature of obsessive thinking. Here, the person holds a belief that the more they think about something the greater the chance is that it will actually happen. For example, the more often they think of themselves being involved in a car accident the more likely it is this will happen. This form of thinking is not so far removed from what is termed magical thinking, that is, a belief that certain actions will have consequences – usually negative.

Superstitions are an everyday example. Many otherwise perfectly rational individuals will not walk under a ladder, or will get upset if they spill milk, or crack a mirror. Spells and other mystical activities are a step up from this and appear to have a profound effect on susceptible individuals. Repeatedly thinking that something will happen sets up an internal conflict between the thoughts themselves and attempts to suppress them. This is one of the root causes of anxiety.

Some Examples of Compulsions

Again, compulsions can involve many different things but in general they will tend to fall into the areas of checking, hoarding, cleanliness and the need to prevent contamination, and symmetry and orderliness. People tend to be much more familiar with these. Examples are frequently shown in real-life documentaries or picked up as humorous or quirky character features of, for example, fictional detectives or writers.

Treatments for Obsessions and Compulsions

Obsessions and compulsions are actually fairly common and many people are able to live with these without their lives becoming disrupted. If lives do become disrupted it is possible that a diagnosis of obsessive-compulsive disorder will be made.

These days, treatments are quite effective and there are many useful self-help strategies that can help to support a formal treatment plan, or be effective in their own right. Whether the treatment is formal (usually via cognitive behavioral therapy) or not, the goal is to try and break into the cycle of obsessive thoughts which lead to feelings of tension and guilt. Compulsive behaviors are the acts or thoughts people use in order to try and neutralize these obsessive thoughts. This may bring about some relief but it is usually short-lived and the cycle repeats itself.

There are basically three treatment options and often these overlap. *Medication*, typically in the form of antidepressants, can be helpful whether or not symptoms of depression are present. *Cognitive behavioral therapy* is an approach that helps people both understand and address the thoughts and behaviors that underpin OCD. Thirdly, there are *self-help* strategies.

Over the years we have learned that gradual exposure to the things or situations that are most feared is one of the best ways to confront the problem. In terms of self-help it means facing the things you fear but in a way that is structured and controllable. It is unusual to find a person with OCD with one and only one issue that makes them ill at ease. Far more likely is a scenario where certain things are most feared and others are least feared but still uncomfortable to have to confront. The principle of exposure therapy is to address the least feared issue first and gradually work towards addressing the most feared issue over time.

As compulsive acts are generally associated with fears it can be helpful to stop carrying out the compulsive acts in order to further break the cycle. Family members or loved ones can help by providing reassurance and you should always remember to praise yourself for avoiding compulsive acts. It is not a good idea to substitute new compulsions for old ones as this is simply like moving pieces on a chessboard. Anxiety is bound to be present as you address these issues but the more often you try the easier things will become until you feel ready to tackle the next fear.

OCD, Men, Anxiety and Depression

There is a significant relationship between obsessive compulsive disorder (OCD) and depression. Estimates suggest around three out of every four people with OCD also experience depression. The exact nature of the association isn't clear but there are some indications that similar mental processes are involved, and biologically, the serotonin system may be implicated.

Men who experience depression often turn to activities as a means of distraction. Sometimes these become compulsive or addictive in nature and they often serve to mask the way they are feeling. When some men become depressed they turn to alcohol and/or drugs. In some respects it might be argued this is a clearer indication of emotional distress than other activities, especially if out of character. But alcohol and drugs aren't the only things men might turn to.

Sometimes compulsive actions come about as a way of filling time, keeping active and relieving anxiety. Compulsive checking, tidying and cleaning are commonplace, but sometimes inner-insecurities are revealed in other ways. Fitness activities can sometimes become compulsive due, perhaps, to the triggering of endorphins that are released during exercise. In these situations the ramifications of not exercising can lead to acute levels of anxiety.

Body-building is another example. I'm not thinking of the average body builder who spends time in the gym after work. I'm thinking more of a condition sometimes known as reverse anorexia or *bigorexia* which reveals itself as compulsive exercising and mirror checking in the belief that the person is physically inadequate. In this condition the man may spend his entire day weight training and exercising, weighing foods, and carefully checking consumption. He may miss social activities and even work because of the compulsive need to train. Yet this is a deeply unhappy person who goes to lengths in order to hide his physique in the belief he is somehow inadequate.

These might be considered extreme forms of compulsion yet other types may be just as hidden. The compulsion to work all hours or to have sex with as many people as possible is just as problematic. In the case of anxiety disorders or depression it is as important to treat the co-existing condition, usually at the same time if the outcome is to be therapeutically effective.

Panic

The so-called anxiety attack is really the culminating moment of excessive worry over an issue. The symptoms, whilst somewhat similar to a panic event (panic attack), do differ enough to distinguish the two.

Despite extensive revision for the exams, Linda feels poorly prepared. Outside the examination hall the other students chatter and laugh nervously. With just minutes to go before the start, Linda begins to feel agitated. Her muscles begin to tense and her legs go rigid. Her hands begin to shake and the more she tries to control the sensations the worse they seem to get. She feels dizzy, sick and short of breath.

The kind of symptoms that Linda feels are severe enough for her to be noticed. A few calming words of reassurance will probably be sufficient for her to settle and within a few minutes she will be able to confront the situation she so dreaded. Once seated, and with the examination underway, the stressor passes and so does the anxiety. This may be the one and only time that Linda goes through such an experience, or, it may be the precursor to other situations or events she associates with stress.

Anxiety attacks and panic attacks can appear so similar that some people appear to have stopped distinguishing between the two. In the case of a panic attack it is the lack of any specific build up to the moment of panic and the level of intensity, which tends to be far more severe. The person who suffers a panic attack may have all of the symptoms previously outlined and more besides. A panic attack may appear to come out of the blue and with such severity the person feels they are going crazy and are about to die. There is a genuine fear of dying and the symptoms are quite frequently misinterpreted as a heart attack, often leading to an emergency hospital admission.

People who experience panic attacks tend to misinterpret bodily signs and focus very much on the moment whereas those who experience anxiety attacks have very specific worrying events in their life that have built up and reached a critical point. The build up is slow, the nature of the anxiety is known, and the symptoms of the attack less intense.

The four most commonly reported symptoms of panic are rapid heart, sweating, dizziness and shortness of breath. People who suffer with shortness of breath often go to great and frequently unpopular lengths, to ensure a supply of fresh air is available. They may, for example, drive with the window down in all weathers. They may insist that windows are always open in the house, or their place of work. The perception of such people as 'fresh air freaks' is a price many are prepared to accept in order to mask the real reason behind their need.

Hyperventilation

Over-breathing (hyperventilation) is as much a cause as it is a feature of panic. Typically this occurs in the form of rapid and fairly shallow breathing which can quickly lead to dizziness and/or light-headedness, plus other symptoms like tingling in fingers, a sense of pressure in and around the chest and a red face. Little wonder these symptoms are frequently viewed as a heart attack both by the victim and sometimes by onlookers.

Assuming a heart attack or other conditions have been ruled out the person may be referred for psychological assessment. As part of the assessment process the person may be asked to undertake a hyperventilation test. This will not be conducted if the person has a medical background of epilepsy, high or low blood pressure, cardiovascular disease or asthma. The test will also be omitted if the person is pregnant.

If conducted, the test will help the therapist determine whether hyperventilation is a key cause of panic. The therapist asks the patient to breathe in a rapid and shallow fashion for up to two minutes. Some form of anxiety assessment may precede the hyperventilation test. This typically involves a rating scale of 0-10 or 0-100 where the upper figure represents absolute fear or terror. Following the test the patient re-rates their anxiety. Usually the second rating reveals a higher level of anxiety and the patient reports very similar sensations to their previous experience of panic.

Some people are prone to repeated hyperventilation and two groups of people appear most affected. The first of these are asthma sufferers (previous and current) and the second are people who, for whatever reason, have a fear of suffocation. The conventional wisdom of asking the person to breathe into a paper bag is based on the reasoning that carbon dioxide is too low as a result of over-breathing. In reality this technique is rarely if ever taught now. One reason is that people in a state of panic are rarely capable of breathing into a bag and secondly there are some medical concerns as to whether the technique is actually counter-productive, particularly if confused with an asthma attack. In practice it is far more common for the person to be taught how to control and regulate their breathing.

Parenting

What makes a good parent? Some people feel it's the most natural thing in the world but for others it feels more like a case of trial and error. Every new generation of parents lives in a world that is often quite different to that experienced by their parents.

Not so long ago people looked to outside experts for guidance on how best to raise our children. Dr. Benjamin Spock is the most notable example. Spock sold over 50 million copies of his book *Baby & Child Care* and quite literally became a legend in his own lifetime. It's easy to forget quite how much Spock's ideas changed the way people viewed parenting. Spock gave parents permission to be their own experts in the way they nurtured and brought up their children. Later in his life Spock would be accused by some of fostering a new generation of spoiled and self-centered children.

Today, psychologists talk about parenting styles and how these have a bearing on the development of the child. Parenting styles can be classified into three broad types. The 'permissive parenting style' is characterized by a lack of boundary setting or the requirement that behavior is appropriately mature. Secondly, the 'authoritarian parent' is emotionally cold, inflexible and frequently severe in dealing with perceived errors or bad behavior. Thirdly, the 'authoritative parent' sets clear boundaries but they are also responsive to needs, supportive and assume high standards of behavior (e.g. Baumrind, 1991).

In relation to the development of anxiety in children, the spotlight has fallen on the effect of parenting styles. Harvard psychologists Jerome Kagan, Ph.D., and Doreen Arcus, Ph.D., well known researchers in the field of child development, say that 'parents' actions affect the probability of anxiety disorder in the child'. Kagan states that the parents in their study are all middle-class and loving but within that context, 'two philosophies are represented. One is, 'I have a sensitive child that I must protect from stress.' So this parent, finding the child playing with rubbish tends not to set limits with a firm 'Don't do that,' but distracts the child. As a result, the child does not get the opportunity to extinguish the fear response." Kagan contrasts this with the authoritative parent who has no difficulty in lifting the child's hands out of the trash and saying 'No. No rubbish', in which a clear boundary is established.

Can we demonstrate a relationship between this and later adult disorders? Possibly. Michael Liebowitz, M.D., Head of Columbia University's unit for panic disorders, told a meeting of the American Psychiatric Association in Philadelphia that he finds unusually high proportions of panic patients say they had overprotective parenting in childhood.

Research to emerge from parenting styles shows a remarkably consistent pattern in the way children develop. For example, children whose parents are authoritative rate themselves, and are rated by objective measures, as more socially and instrumentally competent. Children and adolescents from authoritarian families tend to perform moderately well in school and avoid problem behavior, but they have poorer social skills, lower self-esteem, and higher levels of depression. Children and adolescents from indulgent homes are more likely to be involved in problem behavior and perform less well in school, but they have higher self-esteem, better social skills, and lower levels of depression.

Returning to our biopsychology, one of the main reasons people react so strongly to stressful events lies in the fact that negative emotions are stored as memories in the unconscious mind. These implicit or embedded memories are located in an almond shaped area of the brain known as the amygdala. The amygdala is sometimes thought of as the fear centre of the brain and conditions such as anxiety, autism, depression, post-traumatic stress disorder, and phobias are all suspected of being linked to abnormal functioning of the amygdala.

The fact that we can retrieve negative memories so rapidly is part of the problem. What originally evolved as a mechanism to help remind and protect us against genuine threats seems to be over-sensitive in some people and this results in a strong reaction to situations perceived as threatening. If malign memories are stored during childhood they can continue to affect us as adults, even though as adults we may not be conscious of them. Each time stressful experiences are encountered there is an amplification of negative memories, which can dictate our responses.

This in part explains why people who suffer with anxiety find the situation so frustrating. At one level they are entirely aware of the fact that their worries and their emotional and behavioral reactions are way out of proportion to their situation, yet at another level they feel incapable of more adaptive responses. This is the problem of implicit memories. They can affect our moods and interact with our thoughts so that they are irrational and we have no way of knowing why.

Some of the so-called talking therapies specifically try to work with the patient in order to access and redevelop implicit memories. This way the underlying causes of anxiety and depression can be uncovered and coping strategies developed to make them more tolerable.

Perfectionism

Most people won't admit to being an out-and-out perfectionist. For one thing it makes them sound just a little weird and for another it makes them fallible to imperfections. Therefore it's more acceptable and much more common to hear something along the lines of 'I'm a bit of a perfectionist, but only where work is concerned'.

And here's the problem. It's a rare thing to find someone who is a 'work perfectionist' and who can switch off to become someone else at the end of the day. It's far more likely that the issues of the working day intrude into leisure time. Perfectionists are often at work even when they are meant to have days off or take a vacation. They may not have papers or a computer in front of them but their mind is churning over past decisions and actions to a point where quality of life is affected.

There are different aspects to perfectionism that seem to work for or against us. It clearly works to our advantage to know that a surgeon or an aircraft pilot sets high standards for their work. But it isn't helpful for those same people to maintain such precise standards in their family life, where it can lead to dysfunctional relationships.

Not surprisingly, perfectionists are known to worry and to suffer from stress, and there is some evidence to suggest high perfectionists die younger, but only in certain circumstances. For example, psychologist Prem Fry found that perfectionists with type 2 diabetes have a much lower risk of death because of the attention to detail they apply over the management of their disease.

Many people set high standards for themselves yet have perfectly well balanced lives. The real problem is when people start to worry about mistakes. It is the ruminating concerns that something could have been done better, or may have been overlooked, or hasn't properly been finished that gnaw away at some people. This concern with mistakes seems to be a key area that differentiates excellence from perfectionism.

Of central concern to perfectionists is the fear that if they give up their way of thinking and behaving things will start to fall apart. Many have the intellectual insight to know that perfectionism can actually harm performance more than it helps but their sense of self-worth is so integral to perfectionism it's hard to let go.

Posture

If you are someone who worries a great deal there's a good chance that you also look heavy and burdened. The reason for this is that you feel vulnerable, exposed or threatened. As a result your subconscious is doing its thing by trying to protect you. Physically you may have a tendency to curl inwards when you sit. When you stand your tension may show in hunched or slumped shoulders, a lowered head and curved back. Poor posture has far reaching consequences for both body and mood.

Sitting, standing and walking correctly can take a little practice if you aren't used to it. It can be helpful to check the mirror to see how you stand normally, or even better, get someone who knows about posture (a physiotherapist, yoga instructor, physical trainer) to offer you some feedback. Is it worth all the effort? Yes, is the short answer and here are some of the reasons why:

- in people who are anxious, or prone to panic, their breathing is often quite shallow and often a little rapid.
- a slumped posture increases chest compression and the full capacity of the lungs is under used.
- during stressful moments there is a danger of over-breathing which leads to chest pressure, light-headedness, tingling and increased heart rate. In some people these bodily sensations may be misinterpreted, leading to panic.

Sitting correctly immediately opens the airways and improves circulation. The importance of an effective circulation, feeding organs and the nervous system with necessary oxygen, should not be under-estimated. Very often a few small changes is all that's required:

- in a typical upright chair, ensure your lower back is supported and that you are sitting with your back straight and shoulders back
- ensure your body weight is distributed evenly and that your feet are flat to the floor
- if you can, adjust the height of the seat so that the tops of your legs are parallel to the table you are working with
- try not to remain in a static seated position for more than around 30 minutes

Good posture works wonders with self-confidence. In 2009, a study reported in the European Journal of Social Psychology, illustrated just how influential posture could be. Volunteer job applicants were asked to complete their mock application forms adopting a slumped sitting or upright posture. The findings revealed that those who slumped were less effective in listing their perceived strengths and less likely to articulate why they should be considered a good candidate for the post.

In the treatment of anxiety and panic, quite a lot of attention is given to posture and correct breathing. I don't think there is a therapeutic approach around that doesn't, in some way, indicate the importance of these components. It's good to develop the habit of checking your posture several times a day. When standing:

- keep your shoulders back but relaxed
- pull your stomach in order to stop your lower back curving inward
- don't allow your head to droop
- don't weight bear on one leg
- keep you legs straight when standing but don't lock your knees

The simple act of changing your posture and breathing pattern can quickly change your mood. Breathing steadily and smoothly through the nose quickly helps to relax the body and improve mood.

Yoga

If, like me, you don't know your *mountain pose* from your *fish posture*, then it's clear that yoga has passed you by. However, if you'd like to improve your mood and lessen your anxiety naturally, yoga may be just the thing for you.

One thing I do know a little about is gamma-aminobutyric acid (GABA) and this is the key to what we might call the yoga effect. Yoga is said to increase levels of GABA, so to understand its significance it helps to know a thing or two about GABA.

GABA is a naturally occurring substance found in the brain. It is a neurotransmitter that has a specific role in the anxiety response. The main action of GABA is one of inhibiting nerve cells from firing. Low levels of GABA means high levels of activity between nerve cells, all of which results in the fight-or-flight response associated with stress. Put another way, low levels of GABA lead to high levels of fear.

The effect of benzodiazepine drugs such as Diazepam (Valium) is to enhance the action of GABA, which in turn reduces levels of anxiety. Similarly, alcohol is known to enhance the action of GABA within the hypothalamus and sympathetic nervous system. The problem with alcohol is that it also has the effect of reducing natural production of GABA and this can easily lead to dependence on alcohol in order for the person to maintain their desired emotional state. Although stopping alcohol may be uncomfortable to begin with, the good news is that natural levels of GABA are eventually re-established.

But back to yoga. Researchers at the Boston University School of Medicine (BUSM) have been reporting interesting findings with yoga for some time. In 2007, they published findings in the Journal of Alternative and Complementary Medicine, suggesting that depression and anxiety could be relieved through the practice of yoga. The group compared levels of GABA in volunteers prior to and after one hour of yoga and compared the results with another group of volunteers who sat and read for the same amount of time. A 27 percent increase in GABA was observed in volunteers who undertook yoga.

More recently, the researchers compared yoga with walking and other forms of exercise. Once again they found that yoga had a greater positive effect. The conclusion is that yoga postures seem to stimulate specific areas of the brain associated with GABA production. Quite how the mechanism works and how sustainable the effects are have yet to be fathomed. Still, as an alternative or possibly even a supplement to drugs, it clearly appears to have merit for further investigation. Meanwhile, there's nothing stopping any of us getting involved in this natural and useful form of exercise and relaxation.

Resilience

These days everyone is talking and writing about resilience. Resilience is that aspect of the human condition that enables us to bounce back from adversity, grow stronger from negative experiences and which prepares us to cope with unforeseen challenges.

Thomas Edison once said, 'I haven't failed. I have identified 10,000 ways this doesn't work.' It's a statement of resilience and as much as it's one of those character traits certain lucky people are born with, I'm happy to report that resilience is a skill that we can all learn and profit from. With greater resilience comes:

- confidence, emotional stability and a belief that challenges are manageable
- energy
- openness to new ideas and experiences
- more rapid resolution to stress and greater likelihood of calmness
- generalization. That is, if we develop resilience in just one aspect of life its effects tend to spread to others.

Okay, we all want some of this resilience, but let me inform you that you've already got some reserves. Like all of us you must have experienced setbacks and challenges and yet here you are. My point is that resilience isn't about being Teflon-coated and neither is it about happiness, although that may be a useful spin-off. It's really about coping, but sometimes in different and more adaptive ways than you might be used to.

The way you go about developing resilience is actually a very personal thing. I can offer a few suggestions but what might work for me may mean nothing to you. However, much of what builds resilience is, in some way or another, spread about this book and that explains why some of the following may look a little familiar.

- Problems, fall into two camps, namely issues that can be solved and those that can't. Life circumstances aren't always pleasant but your objective must be to change how you interpret and respond to them if you see problems as insurmountable.
- Make decisions rather than prevaricate. The more you do nothing the more you create a vacuum into which worry and anxiety will spill. You can't detach from life and wish it wasn't happening. We all make wrong decisions in life but if you stand back just in case you do then things will only worsen.
- Your perspectives will improve just by doing the aforementioned. You know you've lost perspective if your focus is narrow, negative and out of proportion.
- If you are part of a close family you are fortunate as this is a key factor in building resilience. Not everyone is in this position but cultivating friendships and accepting help if and when it is offered is equally as important. On this point, you will find that if you offer your services to others the sense of achievement can be tremendous. I've often heard people say things along the lines of 'I can do it for others but not for myself'. Well this is something I dispute because the skills are there but may be laying dormant so far as your own needs are concerned. So try to use them for yourself.

- Try some relaxation, breathing, mindfulness, yoga, or exercise; they all support resilience.
- Visualise what you want and set goals to achieve it. Small steps towards meeting your goals are better than doing nothing and feeling fearful. Break a big task into smaller achievable steps. Be optimistic and try to accomplish
- Be flexible. New approaches may bring with them strong emotions. Give yourself permission to experience these emotions but also learn times when it is best to avoid them. Stepping back to regroup or relax can be just as important as moving forward.
- Be experimental. Rule things in that work for you and rule out those that don't. As previously mentioned, this is a personal journey. There will be stops and starts, obstructions, smooth paths and rough tracks, but to get to where you want to be this is a route you'll need to take.

Risk Taking

Sometimes, just putting our fears into some kind of perspective can help reduce our anxiety. Risk taking, for example, isn't something we normally associate with very anxious people, whereas risk aversion is. So what exactly are anxious people so afraid of?

Really we're talking about fear that has no particular basis in reality, or if it does, the odds are so extreme as to be ruled out. Yet anxious people take risks all the time, probably without even realizing it, and this is where it gets interesting. Did you know there is a 1 in 2 million chance of dying after falling out of bed? Yet we all get out of bed in the morning. There is a 1 in 8 thousand chance of being killed in a road accident, yet most of us still go out and about. Accidental injuries increase our risk to 1 in 36, yet the top three highest odds of death during our lifetimes are heart disease (1-in-5), cancer (1-in-7) and stroke (1-in-23).

I suspect most of us have some level of concern over these last three issues but despite the challenging statistics most anxious people aren't preoccupied with such concerns. So we're back to perspectives and the fact that no matter how we might try, every time we change a light bulb, walk up stairs, use a knife or take a shower, we take risks.

Avoiding harm isn't necessarily to do with physical issues when we're anxious. More likely it's about anticipating the worst, lack of certainty, and dealing with other people. Even decision-making can become an issue if there's the possibility of a less than desirable outcome. Another way of thinking about this is that anxiety tends to be related to risk avoidance whereas confidence is positively related to risk taking.

We don't need to know the statistics in order to challenge ourselves over the perceived risk of some action. We can simply ask ourselves a few modestly searching questions like, what is the evidence that my fear will occur? If it does, what is the worst that could possibly happen? What's an alternative way of looking at this? What would I say to a friend if they revealed their risk-avoiding behaviors?

Building self-confidence undermines risk aversion so remember to do things that support confidence. Dress in a way that makes you feel good about yourself, focus on your strengths rather than your perceived limitations, take care of your body by eating a healthy and balanced diet. Set small challenges that are achievable, for example you might cook for a friend, join a club, or increase your activity levels through exercise. Avoid people and situations that make you feel bad about yourself and set about doing things you enjoy.

Gaining perspective is often to do with tipping the scales to your advantage. As confidence grows and you feel better about yourself, so your aversion to risks in life will start to diminish.

Social

When I say social I'm thinking of social phobia and self-consciousness. Self-consciousness is actually key to understanding how the mind of someone with social phobia works. They can become so preoccupied with how they look, how they are dressed, the way they are standing, sounding and so on that they can't focus properly on what's happening around them. Everything they are trying to avoid seems to conspire against them. The last thing the person with a social phobia wants is attention being drawn to him or herself themselves, yet this is actually more likely. They may shake and their voice may tremble. They may look uncomfortable and sweaty. They may become clumsy and knock into things. It's a vicious cycle that may result in attention from other people.

Hyper-awareness keeps the problem simmering for three reasons. First, it creates a vicious cycle. It makes the social situation appear dangerous and so the need to escape or seek safety increases. Secondly it hinders normal social interaction because the person with a social phobia tends to transmit 'keep away' messages with their body language. Being so self-conscious and self-absorbed can come across as disinterest or aloofness. Thirdly, awareness of other people's needs diminishes. Self-consciousness leaves little space for picking up the cues of say a disappointed expression when someone tries to communicate. Even positive expressions from others can be completely overlooked.

So the question is, what is going on in the mind of this self-consciousness individual? Invariably they will be clustered around negative predictions and assumptions. They will be feeling they don't belong, they aren't liked, they'll do something stupid and show themselves up, or if they do get involved in a conversation they'll run out of things to say. All these are reflective of some very fundamental beliefs the person holds. The problem, which becomes embedded within the vicious cycle, is that the more any of us think we are different to other people the more this is influences our thoughts and behaviors.

What Prolongs the Problem?

The first issue is one we've all experienced and it relates to picking over the bones of previous social encounters. It's those times when we reflect on the things we said and might have said better. It's when we wished we'd behaved this way rather than that, dressed in those clothes rather than these, kept our mouth shout, and so forth. We place ourselves in a no-win situation where we amplify our memory of events and feel embarrassed. Now scale that experience up a few-fold and imagine it on a daily basis and you begin to get an idea of what is happening inside the head of someone with a social phobia.

It's the effects of these thought processes that are so damaging. For a start they feed into the belief the person holds that they are social incompetent and an embarrassment to themselves and others. Their memory of events is also affected by their anxiety to the extent they recall what they *think* happened and this serves to reinforce they negative view they hold about themselves.

People with social phobia are often long-suffering. They are the kind of person who won't, or will never have considered reaching out for help. They shy away from new experiences, live a constrained, controlled and predictable life and as a result are low in confidence. It's lack of confidence that I want to mention as the second issue that prolongs the problem. Unfortunately confidence only builds as we try new things out and accept that mistakes may be made. In reality far more positive outcomes tend to arise from trying out new experiences and this quickly builds confidence.

Finally I want to mention low moods and depression. Many people with social phobia suffer with low moods or depression. It's reasonable to assume that if low moods come about after social phobia symptoms set in that the phobia is the likely cause of the depression. Not surprisingly when people with social phobia work to overcome their low confidence and treat their condition low moods tend to subside.

What Maintains it?

It isn't easy to overcome social phobia but like most things we can take the edge off the problem, and start the process of healing, by understanding what makes a social phobia tick.

The three essential ingredients we need to consider are (1) self-consciousness (2) ways of thinking and (3) ways of behaving that help us feel safe. These three elements will be embedded within situations we find troubling. So, for a situation to be troubling we first need a trigger, that is, something that gets the ball rolling and which will lead to the symptoms associated with social phobia.

Remember Jake in the *Differences* Chapter? Maybe you skipped ahead so to summarise, Jake is a 30 year old social phobic who can't connect with attractive people of the opposite sex. He feels self-conscious, he stumbles over his words, he blushes and inevitably finds a quick reason to get away. Let's unpack the processes underpinning his phobia:

First there's the **trigger**. In Jake's case it will be something like finding himself in a situation where he's speaking to a woman he finds attractive. This activates the **beliefs** and **assumptions** he holds about such encounters. Maybe he thinks he's unattractive both physically and socially? Maybe he feels nothing he says will be of the slightest interest? In activating these beliefs Jake sees **danger** in the situation and perhaps fears he'll be shown up or laughed at. He becomes rapidly and increasingly **self-conscious**. His thoughts become muddled, he feels tense and shaky and he begins to blush. His safety **behaviors** kick in. He avoids eye contact, says as little as possible and looks for reason to get away. Jake is as uncomfortable as he can be. His heart is racing he's sweating, tense and fidgety. In short, he is experiencing the **symptoms** of social phobia.

Jake's experiences may not be shared by others in a similar situation. Jake's way of coping is to avoid eye contact and say as little as possible but another person may speed-talk, filling any potential space by babbling away about anything and everything.

Spots

Does this sound familiar? 'I know exactly what will happen, I'll wake up on the morning of the interview/my date/my audition with a huge red spot on my nose.' For some people their skin seems to act as a barometer of how they feel inside. Sometimes of course the predictions of hair loss, baldness, rashes or spots simply don't come to fruition, but sometimes they seem to. So does stress cause spots and other skin conditions or not?

The first thing we've all probably noticed is that some people can be under enormous levels of stress yet nothing, not even a tiny pimple, blemishes their otherwise perfect skin. Others have very different experiences. Another thing is that plenty of middle-aged and older adults still get spots, so the idea that spots are a curse reserved teens is simply wrong. It's self evident that spots and various skin conditions affect some people and not others. This points to the fact that some people are, for whatever reason, predisposed. So what do we know?

When people are under stress they release more of the stress hormone cortisol. This has the effect of increasing oil production in the body and that can result in a bout of acne, even in adults who may never have experienced it before. According to the American Academy of Dermatology stress makes the skin more sensitive and more reactive. Stress, they say, makes psoriasis or rosacea worse and acne becomes more inflamed and persistent. Brittle and ridged nails are also signs of stress as are hives, excessive perspiration and hair loss. The Academy also points out that skin neglect sometimes comes with stress, so scratching, rubbing, pulling and picking act to increase problems that already exist.

But that still doesn't tell us whether stress actually causes acne. When Dr. Alexa Kimball from Stanford University followed 22 students with acne through their exams, she found that acne worsened as self-reported levels of stress increased. Dr. Kimball also accounted for their sleep patterns, diet, and number of meals in a day, but the most she could conclude was that increasing stress exacerbates acne. A point of interest here is the fact that many people have suggested that stress and acne have something of a circular relationship. That is, stress makes or causes spots and acne worse, which results in more stress, which makes the skin worse still. During Dr. Kimball's study she noted that high achieving populations tend to be less concerned about their appearance during examinations, so perhaps this casts a shade of doubt over the vicious circle theory?

Apart from cortisol, spots are thought to result from other hormones such as testosterone, which is most apparent in teenagers. It is estimated that around 80 percent of adult acne occurs in women around the time of their period, pregnancy or as a result of polycystic ovary syndrome. Steroid medications and lithium, used in the treatment of certain mood disorders can also result in acne.

Acne myths include dirty skin, poor hygiene, sexual activity and chocolate. Although there is some debate about the role of certain diets most experts do not subscribe to the idea that diet has a role in acne.

It seems safe to conclude that stress may not, of itself, be a cause of spots or acne but it does seem to have a role in making things worse. Clinical psychologist and dermatologist Richard G. Fried, MD says when dermatologists treat both the skin and stress, the skin often clears more quickly as the influence of stress is diminished.

The message seems to be that stress reduction techniques such as relaxation, yoga or meditation, coupled with exercise and a balanced lifestyle will all help to reduce the effects of stress, which in those vulnerable to spots, may help to reduce its worse effects and make the duration of outbreaks shorter.

Technology

The dream of technology setting us free has turned into something of a nightmare – or maybe I'm just betraying my age. Technology promised to speed our work, help us make fewer mistakes, enhance our lives and increase our free time.

In my lifetime we've moved from a situation where work was work, and free time began when work finished. It made things very simple and the demarcation lines were clear for all to see. Today, we're having expert seminars on the importance of work-life balance. Is it just a little alarming that we're having to be taught that free time is important?

We're besotted with technology. Access to mobile devices and the internet is viewed by many as a basic need. There are now people on the planet who've never physically written a letter or a memo, except by email. And the days when memo's slowly stacked up on the desk and you took a fortnight to answer them have gone. Happy days!

Work now travels around with us. The day off is becoming an increasingly odd concept and worst of all, away from the devices, the texts and emails, some people get really anxious. It's a curious thing. Technology often provides the illusion of freedom that allows us to do things when we want. In reality our quality of life is gradually eroding because of the technology we love.

Quality of Life & Personal Identity

What do we have in the way of measuring quality of life? Actually there are lots of ways, but I'm turning to the State of Butan for this measure, simply because I love it. How many other countries can you think of that use a measure of 'gross national happiness' in order to measure the well-being of the nation? Brilliant! Effectively it averages out seven 'well-being metrics' that include physical, mental, work, social, economic, political and environmental aspects of well-being. Bhutan in fact ranked eighth out of 178 countries in subjective well-being and is the only country in the top 20 "happiest" countries that has a very low GDP.

Some psychologists and social observers say we're probably much more resentful and unhappy than ever before, despite the affluence many of us enjoy. The build up of daily resentments, sarcasm, cynicism and stress are a toxic mix. The upshot of this is that we're increasingly less open, less approachable, more anxious and more hostile. A possible consequence is that it becomes easier to gain sometimes hundreds of "friends" on social networking sites. We can wear our hearts on our sleeve as easily as we can toss people to one side in this anonymous world.

Does technology fuel our interests and needs or does it simply meet them? Online messaging, tweets and texts create the illusion of community, but face-to-face community takes a bit of effort and is ultimately a more enriching and rewarding experience. Jim Taylor, Ph.D., wonders whether technology is beginning to steal our self-identities? He makes the case that most social forces in previous generations were largely positive: parents, peers, schools, communities and even the media.

Professor Taylor argues that, 'today, popular culture manufactures "portraits" of who it wants us to be. The problem is that the self-identity that is served by popular culture serves its own best interests rather than what is best for us.' It follows that people heavily involved in social media start to see their identity in terms of what they would like it to be and what they feel others want to see. The development of our own personality takes second place as we conform to the requirements of a digital world.

I know technology for some people is life enhancing and sometimes even life critical. For others, does their use of technology help to diffuse responsibility, lower expectations, reduce effort and ultimately make them unhappy and more bitter? It's a big debate and no doubt people have strong views about the role and nature of technology in people's lives.

Mobile Devices

My nephew has a Homer Simpson ringtone. It's configured so that when he receives a call from work it goes 'd'oh!' but when it's from a friend or family it goes 'woo-hoo!' It makes us laugh and it's useful because it acts as a filter. Unless he's expecting an especially important call the one's from work are ignored during his free time.

Our phones and other mobile devices have increasingly become a part of our very fabric. So much a part in fact, that in 2008 the term nomophobia was conjured to reflect the fear and anxiety of being without them. Nomophobics are those people who can't be without their cellphone, who can't switch it off at night, who check for texts or messages several times an hour and who get physical symptoms like increased heart rate and sweating if their phone goes missing.

I may be accused of being picky when I suggest the anxiety connected with loss of a mobile phone doesn't really fall into the phobia category. To me, the need for cellphone use and checking is more a sign of dependency that can lead to compulsive checking acts. In saying that I'm signed up to the idea that phone use does, in some form, act as a barometer of anxiety but the reasons vary from person to person and our age makes a difference too. Loss of a phone may well cause great anxiety but again I think there are a host of reasons why. Maybe the stats for so-called nomophobia have increased because our mobile devices are now more expensive, more complex, contain more personal information, photographs, video's and documents than they ever did, or could, in 2008?

Even so, I think they are great. They can provide us with maps, tell us where the nearest coffee place is, take pictures, contain addresses and pretty much anything we used to consider as the exclusive function of the home computer. It's rare to embrace a technology without finding some darker side in terms of the costs we must pay. For example, there's the use of a phone as a surveillance device. But are mobile devices helpful for anxiety or do they make things worse?

The days when an older child might step out of the door and be told what time they need to be back for dinner have pretty much passed. Today, kids and teens may still go off for the day, but the mobile phone is likely to be with them. Not uncommonly their very first phone will be a gift from parents who view the device as a means of keeping in touch and ensuring everything is o.k. To what extent does the child pick up the message that their phone is a gift because their parents are concerned about their welfare?

The person with the mobile phone quickly realizes it can be used for a whole variety of reasons, one of which is when anxiety strikes. Maybe they call when walking alone, or in a taxi, or in a crowd of people they don't know or feel uncomfortable with. Sometimes, rather than learning to cope with social situations or even a touch of boredom, the phone is available as a handy form of displacement or distraction.

The fact that mobile devices are also used to connect to social media brings a whole new set of issues into the worrying frame. Every day, for example, we learn of vulnerable young people becoming the victims of so-called troll abuse and bullying.

Thinking

Anxiety thinking is a difficult thing to shake off. Some of the beliefs that underpin the thoughts have been developed and refined from a very young age and run so deep that you may find it hard to see them in yourself. Consider the following as to how they might apply to you:

- you tend to make your mind up quickly about situations and have difficulty remaining neutral or considering other options.
- if you make a mistake you see it as a sign that you can't do anything right.
- you feel you know when another person thinks badly of you.
- you often feel embarrassed or responsible for the behavior and actions of those around you.

These are just a few characteristics of anxiety or negative thinking. Anxiety thinking tends to nullify the fact that every situation has a number of possible interpretations.

- that's terrible and it's likely to get worse.
- utterly pointless, I don't know why I bother.
- why hasn't he answered my text? What's wrong?
- this freckle looks big – skin cancer maybe?

Therefore, assuming the worst is a central feature of catastrophic thinking. Of course it's all about context and the belief you have in the things you are saying, rather than the exaggerations we sometimes use in everyday conversation.

Anxious Thinking: Eight Common Errors

When we are anxious we tend to process information differently. We tend to develop a certain bias towards situations and events we find stressful or anxiety provoking, and this basic mechanism is so automatic we can't really see it for what it is. Therapists will often spend time pointing out so-called cognitive errors in an attempt help people see things in a more balanced fashion. In this post I'm outlining eight common cognitive errors. By far the most important of these is catastrophizing or catastrophic thinking.

Catastrophizing is about things growing out of all proportion. Typically something like a small error or a mistake will be seen as having devastating consequences.

Filtering, sometimes called selective abstraction, is about disregarding evidence to the contrary. It's about only seeing the bad but not the good, or highlighting personal weaknesses but not strengths.

Labelling is a form of over-simplistic thinking in which events that have occurred to your disadvantage are viewed as a mirror of personal inadequacies. For example, when missing out on a promotion, the label you apply to yourself might be 'because I'm useless'. This 'explanation' is no more than pointlessly beating yourself over the head with words. The fact that the job went to someone who was more senior, possibly better qualified and more suited, is information overlooked.

Overgeneralizing is about reading too much into situations. The fact you forgot something when shopping turns into proof you are a bad mother. You buy a present that is too big and it becomes evidence how useless you are at everything you try to do.

Mind reading is more of an issue in people who are socially anxious. You firmly believe you know what other people are thinking about you. You actually 'know' they are thinking bad thoughts. Of course the reality of the situation is you can't possibly read the mind of another person. You are interpreting – and your thoughts are your own.

Black and white thinking is also common with low moods and depression. It's a way of seeing things as all good or all bad. If something isn't wonderful it must be terrible. The really unhelpful thing about black and white thinking is that very few things measure up to the 'wonderful' category, so quite a lot of time is spent thinking things are awful.

Fortune telling is that aspect of thinking where we imagine what *might* happen and then we respond emotionally as if it actually *has* happened.

Discounting the positive is certainly one way to hold on to anxious thinking. Ignoring evidence that doesn't fit with our view of the world and ourselves is a feature. If you believe people don't like you and you don't fit in, you'll find it easy to discount situations where people around you are including you. For example, it may very well cross your mind that the only reason they are talking to you is because they feel sorry for you. The idea they find you pleasant, interesting, a good listener, or have other positive qualities will be dismissed.

Negativity Bias and Anxiety

Imagine a situation where we are given one positive piece of information about a person and another that is negative. Which do you suppose we give more weight to? Here's an example. Your boss praises you for a piece of work you've just undertaken and then looks at you in a way that appears critical. Well all the evidence suggests the thing that will prey on your mind is the look. Why? Well it seems part of the human condition that we're wired to pay more attention and give more weight to negative rather than positive emotions.

We take a criticism (implied or otherwise) much more seriously than we take a compliment. Again, why? We have to go right back to our ancient ancestors for the answer. From an evolutionary perspective our modern day lives and lifestyles are really quite recent. You've probably heard the comment that we inhabit our space age in the bodies of cavemen, and that's pretty much the case. While technology has surged ahead our physiology treads water. So we're in a situation where we're still tuned to the strong possibility of threat as a survival instinct. Electrical activity in our brain is stronger to events perceived as negative.

The way we live today such sensitivities largely serve to get in the way of wellbeing. A positive and a negative experience is not equal and don't seem to cancel each other out.

In fact it has been calculated that one negative requires around three or more positives to counteract it. Some relationship experts suggest a ratio of five positives to one negative is necessary for the relationship to survive.

Sad as it may seem we remain more attuned and more affected by bad news, disasters, unhappy faces, goodbyes and losses over gains. A good day lasts a day, a bad day lasts as long as it takes. Estimates suggest that up to two-thirds of our language and even most of our dreams are front-loaded with negativity, worry and anxiety. It has been suggested that our negativity bias leads to more hawkish views for quick-fix revenge over more durable solutions that require finding compromise and concessions.

Does it help to know this? I think so. Without some awareness into our human frailties we expose ourselves to situations that lead to greater anxiety, stress and possibly danger. In any act of communication, whether in a relationship or across political divides, negativity bias inevitably plays a part in our views and our decision-making. It's a big part of us and we somehow have to be bigger in order for harmony to dominate.

Anxiety Interpretations

In any treatment of anxiety disorders the therapist will often stress the significance of interpretations. We are constantly taking stock of our environment, the people and situations we encounter. It doesn't necessarily happen at a conscious level but we can see the significance of interpretations in a variety of ways.

One day I came to the aid of someone with a morbid fear of spiders. She'd called for help from the kitchen where she was rooted to the spot, face half turned from the object of terror, and pointing towards it. What she thought was a large spider lurking in the shadows turned out to be nothing more intimidating than top of a tomato that had dropped to the floor. When this was pointed out it resulted in instant relief and laughter.

The point of the story is that emotional reactions come about as a result of the way we interpret a situation, not the situation or event itself. The significance is personal and in people who are very anxious the significance is usually evaluated as dangerous.

Cognitive therapists know that interpretation is highly significant. In anxiety the form of interpretation is largely centered on the fact that an event is viewed as much more threatening than it really is. Depending on the disorder the content of interpretation will differ. In the case of panic disorder, for example, it is the interpretation of normal bodily functions that causes problems. A fast beating heart may give rise to the belief that a heart attack is imminent. We can contrast this with social anxiety disorder where the content of interpretation is more likely to relate to an intense fear of being judged negatively by other people.

But there are other examples. In OCD, the person is likely to interpret unwanted intrusive thoughts as signs of madness or badness. People with a generalized anxiety disorder may interpret their worrying as a sign they are caring and kind and their worrying is a way of somehow preventing bad things happening.

Interpretations are of course a way of thinking. This simple but fundamental helps inform the principles of cognitive therapy. Interpretations can appear as truths and a big part of cognitive therapy is helping a patient accept that the way they think is an incredibly important feature in helping to promote their anxiety.

Images and Hotspots in Anxiety Disorders

The way we think often involves images rather than words, or sometimes both. Like a movie we play out scenes in our mind and almost like a dream, we can experience the emotional outcomes. A person who is anxious can often generate some dramatic and upsetting negative imagery. What starts out as concern over the length of time their partner has been driving develops into images of him or her falling to sleep behind the wheel and eventually being mangled in some terrible crash.

Images can be truly upsetting. Imagining the loss of a loved one, perhaps because they have rejected you or because they are very ill, is a troubling thing. People with health or social anxieties or those prone to panic often 'see' themselves in situations where they are vulnerable and unable to cope. Reducing such images can be part of treatment and this is certainly something being refined in the treatment of those with post-traumatic stress disorder (PTSD) who experience flashbacks.

Images tend to mean something and it can be helpful for the person affected to unpack the images they see and to verbalize their meaning rather than simply be affected by the emotions they stir. For example, let's imagine that Jimmy has to give a presentation to work colleagues. In the days leading up to the presentation his imagination stirs. He sees himself stumbling over his words, sweating and shaking, and his audience laughing at him. He sees himself running out of the room, humiliated. He feels sick at the thought and his anxiety levels begin to peak.

One way of tackling issues like Jimmy is experiencing is to weigh up the evidence for and against the negative imagery he is generating. The first step is for him to articulate the exact nature of his negative images. In Jimmy's case it's about lack of confidence and, as is often the case with anxious imagery, a memory of a time some years ago when he felt self-conscious because of something he was expected to do in front of others. Next, it would help if he weighs up the evidence both in favor and against these images. Very often it's a case of worry over real hard evidence.

Problematic mental imagery occurs with almost all anxiety disorders but are probably most intense in those suffering with PTSD. Usually the person experiences a worst moment or moments of trauma known as 'hotspots'. These hotspots tend to relate to physical or emotional threat experienced by the person. Trauma focused cognitive therapy involves a technique called imaginal reliving, in which hotspot moments are focused on and recalled. The aim is to allow for better processing of the event and the association it has for the person. For example a hotspot image of being mugged at knifepoint may be associated with the meaning that 'I'm going to die.' Manipulating the concept might lead to a place where the person thinks, 'I know I didn't die.' The interpretation of the event and the sense of 'nowness' that accompanies it, is known to reduce as a result of such approaches.

Exaggeration

From time to time we're all guilty of making a few verbal embellishments to spice up a story. But sometimes, when we're unhappy or stressed, there's a tendency to magnify the negative and discount the positive. It's possible to get trapped in this mode of thought and it can be difficult to move forward. Here are some examples of exaggerated thinking styles and some possible alternatives.

Have you ever found yourself using words like 'disastrous', 'devastated', 'ruined', 'impossible', to describe either the way you feel or situations you're involved in? If so you may be using language to exaggerate situations; a process called catastrophising. Listening to the way people use language is an important way of detecting how they are coping with issues in their life such as rejection, work pressures, failure and the like. So while the use of 'catastrophic' language can say something to others about the level of anxiety a person feels, it can also be an important way to self-monitor our own anxieties and do something about it.

We may not always be able to change the situations we find ourselves in but we can make adjustments to the ways we perceive them simply by making a more conscious effort to modify the language we use. Will it really be 'a disaster' if something isn't done on time, or will it be a nuisance? Do you really find something 'impossible' to do, or might it be useful to ask for a little help to solve the problem? If you feel under pressure, anxious or depressed, try listening to the language you're using. If it does have a 'catastrophic' edge try fine-tuning it to a point where the words and the outcomes are less dramatic. You'll experience less stress and see more options for solutions.

Another example of exaggeration is over-generalization. Here we leak our thinking style through the use of sweeping negative statements that often have little if any basis in evidence. For example, can someone really 'always' be wrong? Can they 'never' say or do the right thing? If something bad happens once does it really mean you should give up trying because all future attempts are bound to result in failure? If this were true a huge proportion of the population would never find a partner, or pass their driving test, or give up smoking, or ride a bike. So many things in life require some trial and error and a development of skills before we can feel a little comfortable with them. Over generalizing can say something about our anxiety for trying things again. It's a negative thought process that blocks forward movement.

In many ways this example stems from the previous two. It's is a process called labeling where we reach conclusions about ourselves and choose to ignore alternatives. Unfortunately we're as prone to labeling others as we are to ourselves. So if we start to think of ourselves as 'useless', 'stupid', 'idiotic' or 'a loser', we're effectively painting ourselves into a corner and ignoring alternative options. Labeling is a form of stereotyping and we all know how clunky and inaccurate this is. You know the sort of thing, 'all rich people are . . .' 'all drug users are . . .' Life is far too rich and complex for such negative labels, so if you find yourself thinking such self-limiting thoughts it's time to step back and consider the broader picture.

Mindset

Psychologist Carol S. Dweck maintains that people with a fixed mindset are overly focused on performance goals and avoiding failure. When they achieve these goals they feel validated but can still feel anxious because it means they have to work as hard or harder to maintain the status quo. When these often self-imposed standards can't be met the person feels hopeless and helpless.

Dweck contrasts this with a growth mindset in which the person remains open to new ideas, is willing to take a risk on trying something new and doesn't get hung up on issues like winning or losing, or passing or failing.

One thing we can say about fixed mindset folk is they tend to be persistent. When confronted by a problem they typically keep repeating the same behaviour yet hope for a different outcome. They resist trying new ideas and as a result all the negative emotions they carry just follow them around.

One of the techniques Dweck uses to shift the bias towards a growth mindset is to teach people about brain function. We all know we have at least the potential to change and the same is true of our brains. Using our mind to change our brain isn't far fetched and there are plenty of examples to prove the point.

So, let's imagine you're a brain. As you go about your business a worry comes your way, so you fire up a few neurons to respond. But this and other worries go on and on, so you think, 'hang on, this must be really important, I'd better commit more resources to it,' and so you fire up a few more neurons and you start to make more robust and stable connections. Before too long you've established a nice neural structure for your anxieties. Okay, you can stop being a brain now.

As Canadian psychologist Donald Olding Hebb once put it, 'neurons that fire together, wire together' and this tells us something about how we can exert a positive influence over our own brains. Carol Dweck uses this neuroscience knowledge in order to teach people to learn or practice something new in order to develop their brain in new directions. There's nothing complicated about it, but it does require you to acknowledge your mindset may have blocked you from getting what you want or where you want to be. The next step is thinking what you could do differently in order to achieve these goals rather than repeating the same things over and over and getting nowhere.

Fixed mindsets sound more concrete than they actually are. The fact is the brain is like any other muscle and the more you use it and test it and try new things out the better it will perform.

The neuropsychologist Dr. Rick Hanson says that people who routinely relax have improved gene expression that helps calm stress reactions. You'll also be pleased to note that all the relaxation and mindfulness you'll be undertaking has brain benefits in the form of thicker layers of neurons of the pre-frontal cortex. Mindful activity boosts left prefrontal cortex activity, which helps to suppress negative emotions and reduces activation of the amygdala, what Hanson refers to as the "alarm bell of the brain".

Reduced to its basics we can say that the human condition is a product of genes and the environment. We know we have a certain level of control over our environment, but it is often assumed we have no control over our brain or our genes. I've discussed the brain but in any attempt to beat anxiety it is worth knowing that some genes are like switches; we can in fact switch them on and off.

Unfortunately our full understanding of genes in relation to anxiety remains a bit sketchy so the production of a tablet to target and switch off the excesses of anxiety has a few years to go. Anxiety, depression and other mood disorders are known to have a genetic component. Various proteins surround and stick to DNA and part of the role of these proteins and chemicals is to switch genes on and off.

Factors such as diet are known to have a significant role in switching genes on or off. The implication for anyone with a genetic predisposition towards anxiety and depression is that by balancing environmental influences, like diet and other lifestyle issues, protective genes can be switched on while others can be switched off. Foods rich in complex carbohydrates, such as rice, corn, barley, peas and lentils are examples. Complex carbohydrates increase the amount of serotonin in the brain whereas simple carbohydrates do not. Simple carbohydrates are found in sugar, cakes, jams, biscuits and honey and packet cereals, for example.

Of course if it was down to switching to salads, rice and pulses and getting out the rowing machine everyone's troubles would quickly dissipate. Even so, it does rather depend on the depth of the problem. You may find you can achieve complete relief by making changes to your diet and lifestyle whilst or you may feel just a little better.

So, why the differences? Some of the more obvious reasons relate to whether you are male or female. Women, for example, have the burden of having naturally higher levels of stress hormones, while testosterone in men appears to protect against stress.

Early life experiences also appear to have significant effects on the sympathetic nervous system that can affect levels of sensitivity in later life and for the whole of life. We are unable to reverse-engineer our early life experiences but we do have it within our gift to modify their effects.

Our bodies don't discriminate between physical and psychological stress. Stress hormones are as likely to be produced in response to thirst, food additives, caffeine and viral infections as they are to negative emotions. Likewise, a noisy, hot, polluted environment feeds the stress response. Even mild dehydration can affect mood, so drink plenty of water during the day. Alcohol, recreational drugs, and cigarettes, all have negative effects although at the time they may feel as though they are alleviating anxiety or low moods.

Vision

One of the more common effects of anxiety is eyestrain or other forms of visual disturbance. This is nearly always related to the surge in adrenaline that accompanies anxiety and there's no harm in spending just a few moments outlining what's happening.

Primary and secondary forms of anxiety have different effects. *Primary* anxiety is that part of our fight-or-flight system that energizes us to deal with some threat. Our body floods with adrenaline, sugars, fats and other hormones to allow us to take action.

Secondary anxiety, by contrast, has no particular focus. It manifests itself in terms of worry and concerns over whether certain tasks or activities are within the grasp of the individual. It's hard to control, it interferes with performance and it can feed physical symptoms such as shaking, difficulty with walking, nausea, giddiness and distortions with vision.

In the case of chronic stress and anxiety, the level of adrenaline within the body remains elevated. This can cause pressure on the eyes, sometimes resulting in blurred vision. Tunnel vision is another feature of excessive adrenaline. This tends to occur at times of high arousal or during a panic event.

Previously I described the features of hypervigilance; this actually affects all the senses but as far as vision is concerned our pupils dilate in response to adrenaline in order to take in more of our surroundings. We become highly sensitized to any slight movement. Over time this, and the strain from other senses, can cause muscular tensions and headaches.

Some people with long-term anxiety find that wearing tinted lenses or sunglasses reduces light sensitivity. This seems to help with their anxiety and also helps to prevent headaches. Some prescription lenses have permanent tints or are of a type that react to light.

While some level of relief may be achieved this way, not everyone with anxiety wears tinted lenses for the same reason. Dark lenses can also act as a kind of social barrier and while wearing them isn't really a solution to the problem, for some people they clearly seem to have a place. The use of dark or tinted lenses are used as a response to high arousal, so the emphasis should still be on trying to find ways to reduce this state of arousal.

Work

When it comes to anxiety and stress the world of work is often a central focus, partly because it can be such an unforgiving place but sometimes it just seems that way. In our day to day dealings we generally accept a little nervousness in others but employees who exhibit anxiety during business exchanges, presentations or social gatherings send out the wrong message. It's bad for business.

In most work environments people follow codes of accepted behavior. Sometimes these codes take a little while to master. Some are overt and can be embedded as a part of company policy (no shouting or swearing, for example). Others are more subtle and unwritten and involve anything from never using Sally's mug, to the raising of an eyebrow from the boss to signal displeasure.

The thing about a successful interpersonal environment is that it represents a form of trade. You offer me something and I will offer something in return; I offer you a coffee and you accept or graciously decline. These interactions lubricate our social wheels and they encourage us to believe that future interactions will go well. However, if one or both people are anxious it can lead to clumsy or inappropriate statements or behaviors. In turn, this may cause a collapse in the interaction that can lead to embarrassments, further anxiety or even hostility.

Coping with our own anxiety is one thing but coping with other people's anxiety requires additional skills. We can't necessarily see anxiety in other people, but it is often easy to infer. So what are the consequences? Anxiety often comes across as irritation, but if we meet this with our own irritation the situation is more likely to escalate. Then again, if we make attempts to understand their irritation, it can be viewed as patronizing. Therefore, in order to sustain a relationship with anxious people the general rule is to empathize and offer reassurance whilst ensuring you achieve what you need.

This last statement isn't intended to sound heartless but we need to distinguish our role in work. Are we employed to be a therapist or not? Is part of our role to get on with colleagues yet achieve our goals? Probably yes.

Personal anxieties are often fuelled by self-destructive inner conversations about lack of worth, skills and inadequacies. We can chip away at personal anxieties by focusing our energies on behaving in a more relaxed and confident manner. This alone helps some people. For others it's more important that they become involved with the inner conversation as this is the cause of their confidence becoming eroded.

What do I mean by an inner conversation? Well it's all those negative beliefs you hold about yourself, such as the fact you aren't experienced enough, capable enough, or clever enough to express an opinion. It's the beliefs you hold that if you say or do something everyone will think you are stupid. It's the assumption that you may offend, upset, or cause others to laugh at you, and so on.

It was Mark Twain who observed that his life had been full of troubles , but most of them had never happened. We all have strengths and limitations but our self-belief governs which of these dominate our thinking and therefore our anxieties.

Performance Anxiety

So many work roles now require different forms of presentational skill. The everyday term associated with performance related anxiety is stage fright. Although it reveals itself in different ways, people's stage fright fears are really quite consistent. The greatest fear for people is showing signs of anxiety such as trembling or having a shaky voice. Fear of the mind going blank, freezing and being unable to continue, saying or doing something embarrassing or saying something stupid, are also high on the agenda.

In principle, there isn't such a difference between talking to one person and talking to several. Granted, more of a two-way interaction is expected with just two people, but beyond this the difference between say speaking to two or two hundred is a matter of scale and a difference in direction. Whether we talk to one person or to many we engage in a process where both the speaker and those who listen have goals. In a successful delivery, goals are met, but if anxiety inhibits the process neither the speaker nor the audience is satisfied. Anxiety is contagious and it results in frustration.

The root of stage fright is a kind of internal dialogue which becomes handicapping. It goes along the same lines I've previously mentioned, of the person feeling they are not experienced enough or clever enough to do this.

Aside from the actual skill of presentation, the person fears the negative evaluation of others and of being the center of attention. When the person does begin their presentation, they may further handicap themselves by apologizing in advance. It sets up a negative experience for their audience who are left feeling tense on behalf of the speaker and/or concerned they are about to get a poor deal.

Pretty much all the advice you will come across about stage fright says the same thing about the need for preparation. If you haven't got the basics together, you stand a far higher chance of things going wrong.

A useful blog I read on the website Psychologytoday.com was entitled, *Fighting Stage Fright*. The article cites Joseph O'Connor who, it seems, suggests five minutes of preparation for every minute of presentation. Also, speak out loud so that you become accustomed to the sound of your own voice. Time yourself and maybe get someone to listen to you and offer feedback.

In the same article, the author suggests exaggerating your own symptoms. So, if you suffer from shaking, try to make your hands shake more. The author claims you will find that your hands then stop shaking. The principle here is that if you are able to increase symptoms, you are able to control them.

Arriving early at the venue is frequently regarded as a good thing. It allows you to become familiar with the space and the equipment. If you are amongst the first to arrive you effectively 'own' the space that others will then enter. Arrive last and it's a bit like having to enter any crowded space in that, for many people, it's just a little more difficult.

If you have done your preparation, you should find things go pretty smoothly. Nobody expects or even listens out for a slick presentation. How many times have you heard a newsreader have to retrace something they've said? All those years of practice and they're still prone to stumbling and making errors. We all do it, so if you find yourself in the situation, take the time to get back on course and don't get flustered

The Causes, Signs and Symptoms of Work-Related Stress

Work overload can lead to physical and emotional exhaustion that leads to symptoms such as headaches, stomach complaints and difficulties sleeping. We can see the signs of work overload in people when they become inflexible, critical, irritable, and when they deny having a problem. Left to fester, they become cynical, tired, detached and prone to making errors and mental health starts to suffer. These are all signs of burnout.

Work underload is the extreme opposite of burnout yet its effects can be just as marked. A dull, repetitive, unrewarding job with no prospects can quickly lead to boredom. Left unchecked, apathy sets it and productivity slows. Such jobs can become highly stressful as there is no outlet other than grumbling. In worst case scenario's workers may even resort to minor acts of sabotage that can negatively affect products or customers. These are all the symptoms of 'rust-out' previously described.

Fear of job loss during difficult economic times can do strange things to people. They may find themselves turning up earlier than usual for work, taking shorter breaks, staying longer and volunteering for extra work in an attempt to show dedication and perhaps increase their profile. They may refuse to take a day off sick, even when it is needed. Turning into work when sick is called presenteeism and it's a sign of vulnerability and work anxiety.

Workaholics are almost completely preoccupied with work. Work is the top priority and dominates all other considerations including relationships, family and friends. While some workaholics get a buzz from work, others use work to deflect attention from deeper issues such as depression, troubled relationships, or the fear of job loss, or of losing personal control. In such situations excessive patterns of work may mask a developing issue of stress that is simply accumulating and at some point may lead to illness.

Technology is both an asset and a curse. In principle, and often in practice, we are contactable 24 hours a day. Whereas work used to be located in a building that we could walk away from, it now follows us about via email, texts, and various other social media outlets. Some people have found ways to manage this and can divide their time between personal life and work life. Increasingly however there is an expectation, often unstated, that people should be available to meet the needs of work when necessary. The stress of work technology is a relatively new feature and its one that is fueling debates over how it affects our quality of life.

Workplace bullying takes many forms and includes rudeness, spreading gossip, being given impossible deadlines, ageist or sexist comments and more besides. Most of the time we get along with people because we sign up to accepted modes of behavior. We are polite, we try to be helpful, and if we take we try to give back. But people are a pretty mixed bunch and sometimes they don't share this agenda. The effects of bullying are so harmful some experts claim they are worse than sexual harassment.

Signs of work-related stress also tend to vary because of the type of work involved and lifestyles out of work. The most common signs are likely to include the need to work longer hours. A sense that there is never enough time. There's little or no time for relaxation. Rushing to complete things. Missing breaks. Missing vacation entitlements. Spending less time with family and friends.

Symptoms of work-related stress tend to vary because we all react to stress in different ways. However, the most common psychological symptoms include inability to concentrate, loss of motivation, and a lack of confidence and commitment to work. Emotionally, there is a tendency to become more sensitive, more irritable, and to feel more negative or have depressive feelings. This combination of psychological and emotional upsets often shows in physical symptoms that typically include headaches, back pain, digestion and bowel problems. Eating patterns may change, sleep patterns may alter and drinking alcohol or drug use may increase.

More and more stressed workers are turning up to work when they should really be at home recovering. Since the start of the global economic turndown there has been a fall in the number of working days lost due to sickness. In cases where people do take a day or more off sick, the number of cases due to stress has also fallen. So has work suddenly become less stressful or are other factors in play?

Previously I mentioned something called presenteeism (turning into work when sick). There are a couple of reasons why this occurs. The first is that you might be part of a small team, perhaps working in a business that is hanging on by the fingernails. Every single person in the team matters and you know the effect it can have if one or more people aren't around. The burden on colleagues increases and you simply don't want to let the team down. The second reason is more anxiety related. During times of job insecurity there is pressure on managers and their workforce to be ever more competitive. Absenteeism costs money and it's something that is easy to measure and record. If people in a workforce feel vulnerable the last thing they want is to have a poor sickness record. Bluntly put, nobody wants to appear weak in case they lose their job.

Each year, the American Psychological Association (APA) commissions a nationwide stress survey. The Stress in America http://www.apa.org/news/press/releases/stress/index.aspxSurvey reports money (75 percent), work (70 percent) and the economy (67 percent) as the most frequently cited causes of stress. This year, as with previous years, women were more likely to report feeling stressed. Men are less likely than women to believe that stress can affect their health and appear less inclined to recognize stress. Men however are much more inclined to report being diagnosed with diseases that have a clear association to lifestyle and stress. A good number of people still report unhealthy behaviors associated with stress. Sleep problems, skipping meals, irritation and anger and reduced sex drive are most common in younger men, who are also more likely to be stressed by the economy.

According to the APA survey, more adults report that their stress is increasing than decreasing. Nearly 40 percent of those surveyed said their stress had increased over the past year and 44 percent said their stress had increased over the past five years. This is offset to some extent by reports that 27 percent of adults say their stress had decreased over the past five years and 7 percent in the past year.

The problem with presenteeism is that it ultimately becomes hugely costly. An unhealthy workforce results in more errors, more accidents and reduced productivity. The Center for Mental Health makes the point that only a small part of ill health in the workforce is actually caused by work, which on the whole is good for health. A climate of anxiety simply feeds stress, which in turn has a depleting effect. It is therefore in the best interests of companies not to turn the screw too tightly on its workforce if they want to get the best out of them.

Bibliography

Baer, J. C., Kim, M., Wilkenfeld, B Is it Generalized Anxiety Disorder or Poverty? An Examination of Poor Mothers and Their Children. *Child and Adolescent Social Work Journal*, 2012.

Baumrind, D. (1991). The influence of parenting style on adolescent competence and substance use. *Journal of Early Adolescence*, 11(1), 56-95.

Bilkei-Gorzo, A., Erk, S., Schürmann, B., et al. Dynorphins Regulate Fear Memory: from Mice to Men. *The Journal of Neuroscience*, 4 July 2012, 32(27):9335-9343

Bogart, L.M., M. N. Elliott, D. J. Klein, S. R. Tortolero, S. Mrug, M. F. Peskin, S. L. Davies, E. T. Schink, M. A. Schuster. Peer Victimization in Fifth Grade and Health in Tenth Grade. *PEDIATRICS*, 2014; 133 (3)

Brinol, P., Petty, R.E., & Wagner, B. (2009). Body posture effects on self-evaluation: a self-validation approach. *European Journal of Social Psychology, 39,* 1053-1064.

Coplan, J., Hodulik, S., Mathew, S.J., (et al) The Relationship between Intelligence and Anxiety: An Association with Subcortical White Matter Metabolism. *Frontiers in Evolutionary Neuroscience*, 2012: 3 DOI: 10.3389/fnevo.2011.00008

Deschênes, S.S., Dugas, M.J., Fracalanza, K., Koerner. N (2012) The Role of Anger in Generalized Anxiety Disorder. Cognitive Behavior Therapy. 2012;41(3): 261-71.

Eluvathingal, T.J., Chugani, H.T., Behen, M.E., et al. Abnormal brain connectivity in children after early severe socioemotional deprivation: a diffusion tensor imaging study. *Pediatrics*. 2006;117: 2093–100.

Freudenberger, Herbert; Richelson Géraldine (1980). *Burn Out: The High Cost of High Achievement. What it is and how to survive it.* Bantam Books.

Han-Joo Lee, Jesse R. Cougle, Michael J. Telch (2005) Thought-action fusion and its relationship to schizotypy and OCD symptoms. Behaviour Research and Therapy 43. 29-41.

Fry, P. S. Perfectionism and other related trait measures as predictors of mortality in diabetic older adults: A six-and-a-half-year longitudinal study. *Journal of Health Psychology* 16 (7) 1058-1070.

Gorzo, A., Erk, S., Schurmann, B (et al) Dynorphins Regulate Fear Memory: From Mice to Men. The *Journal of Neuroscience* DOI: 10.1523/JNEUROSCI.1034-12.2012

Hofman, S.G., Moscovitch, D.A., Litz, B.T., Kim, H.J., Davis, L.L. & Pizzagalli, D.A. (2005). The worried mind: autonomic and prefrontal activation during worrying. *Emotion*, 5(4), 464-75.

Kiecolt-Glaser, J., Glaser, R., Gravenstein, S., Malarkey, W., & Sheridan, J. (1996). Chronic stress alters the immune response to influenza virus vaccine in older adults. Proc. Natl. Acad. Sci., 93, 3043–3047.

Kiecolt-Glaser, J. K., McGuire, L., Robles, T. F., & Glaser, R. (2002). Emotions, morbidity, and mortality: New perspectives from psychoneuroimmunology. Annu. Rev. Psychol.,53, 83–107.
Ogden, J (2012) Health Psychology a textbook (5th ed) Open University Press, McGraw-Hill Education.

Pennebaker, J.W. (1997) Writing About Emotional Experiences as a Therapeutic Process. *Psychological Science*. Vol 8. 3. 162-166

Pennebaker, J.W., & Seagal, J.D. (1999) Forming a Story: The Health Benefits of Narrative. *Journal of Clinical Psychology* 55 (10) 1243-1254.

Pennebaker, J.W., & Chung, C.K. (2007) Expressive Writing, Emotional Upheavals, and Health. In H. Friedman and R.Silver (Eds), *Handbook of Health Psychology* (pp. 263-284). New York: Oxford University Press.

Phillips, K.A., Coles, M.E., Menard, W., et al. Suicidal ideation and suicide attempts in body dysmorphic disorder. *Journal of Clinical Psychiatry*. 2005 Jun; 66(6): 717-25.

Phillips, K. A., Menard, W. Suicidality in Body Dysmorphic Disorder: A Prospective Study. *American Journal of Psychiatry* . 2006 163 (7): 1280–2.

Lederbogen, F., Kirsch, P., Haddad, L. (et al.) City living and urban upbringing affect neural social stress processing in humans. *Nature*, 2011; 474 (7352): 498

Rachman, S (2004) Anxiety. Psychology Press.

Rai, D., Kosidou, K., Lundberg, N., Lewis, G. Psychological distress and risk of long-term disability: population-based longitudinal study. *Journal of Epidemiology & Community Health*, 2011.

Schoenfeld, T.J., Rada, P., Pieruzzini, P.R., Hsueh, B and Gould, E. P. Physical Exercise Prevents Stress-Induced Activation of Granule Neurons and Enhances Local Inhibitory Mechanisms in the Dentate Gyrus. *The Journal of Neuroscience*, 1 May 2013, 33(18): 7770-7777.

Taylor, J (2011) Is Technology Stealing Our (Self) Identities? *Psychology Today*. http://www.psychologytoday.com/print/70307

Taylor, S. E., Klein, L. C., & Lewis, B. P., Gruenewald, T.A. (2000). Biobehavioural response to stress in females: tend-and-befriend, not fight-or-flight. *Psychological Review*, *107*(3), 411-429.

Tomova, L., B. von Dawans, Heinrichs, M., Silani, G., Lamm. C. Is stress affecting our ability to tune into others? Evidence for gender differences in the effects of stress on self-other distinction. *Psychoneuroendocrinology*, 2014; 43: 95

Von Dawans, B., Fishbacher, U., Kirschbaum, C., Fehr, E., Heinrichs, M. The social dimension of stress reactivity: acute stress increases prosocial behaviour in humans. Psychological Science, 2012

Wolke, D., Lereya. S.T. Bullying and Parasomnias: A Longitudinal Cohort Study. *PEDIATRICS*, 2014: 2014-1295